The
Spirit

The
Spirit

Who He Is and What He Does

DR. BOB BELTZ

ILLUMIFY
MEDIA.COM

The Spirit

Published by
Illumify Media Global
www.IllumifyMedia.com
"Let's bring your book to life!"

Paperback ISBN: 978-1-964251-87-5

Typeset by Art Innovations (http://artinnovations.in/)
Cover design by Debbie Lewis

Discus thrower discobolus statue on page 102 © Ruslan Gilmanshin
Dreamstime.com

All biblical references are direct translations from the Greek text by the author. Any similarities to other translations is purely coincidental and the result of good scholarship on the part of both the author and the other translators.

Printed in the United States of America

To the Renegade Pastors
Gentlemen and Scholars All

CONTENTS

ACKNOWLEDGMENTS

I would like to express my appreciation to the many people who made this book possible. Although they might not want to take responsibility, thank you to the faculty of Denver Seminary (especially Dr. Donald Burdick, Dr. Kermit Ecklebarger, and especially Dr. Vernon Grounds) who during my days as a student there, gave me the tools that through the years have helped me both to understand and to communicate the critical truths contained within this book.

I'm grateful to the wonderful men and women of five super churches of which I have had the privilege of being a part. First, to Bob Lehleitner and the members of Colonial Presbyterian Church, Kansas City. Second, to Roger Allmand and the people of Trinity Evangelical Free Church, Holdrege, Nebraska. Third, to Dr. Jim Dixon and the congregation of Cherry Hills Community Church, Denver. Fourth, all the folks at High Street Community Church, Santa Cruz, California, and Finally, the staff and people of Highline Community Church, Denver, Colorado.

Thanks to Michael Klassen and the team at Illumify Media for all their hard work in getting this book published.

Finally, thanks to my beautiful wife, Joy. Your love and encouragement infuse and inspire everything I do.

—Bob Beltz

UNDERSTANDING THE NEED

You will receive power when the Holy Spirit
has come upon you.

—Acts 1:8

ON A HOT SUMMER NIGHT in mid-July 1977, the lights went out in New York City. The greatest metropolis in America, and arguably the world, was thrown into chaos. Traffic went into gridlock as the signal lights went black. Commerce came to a screeching halt. Fear gripped the hearts of citizens as bands of looters began roaming the streets. Millions sat paralyzed in the darkness.

What caused such a situation? A power shortage.

Some have referred to the New York event as the greatest power shortage in history. I know of a greater one. It's a power shortage that affects every person on earth.

Over eight billion men and women are immobilized by this shortage. It's a shortage that has thrown not just one city into chaos, but the entire world. It's not a physical power shortage, but a spiritual one.

Listen to the final words of Jesus before His ascension, an incredible promise: "You will receive power . . . " (Acts 1:8). In many ways, this promise was a reminder of things Jesus had taught consistently in the years He had been with His followers. "Apart from me you can do nothing" (John 15:5). To paraphrase—"You are powerless." "Stay in the city until you have been clothed with power from on high" (Luke 24:49). To put it another way—"The task I have for you to accomplish will require a power that you do not yet possess." "No one can see the kingdom of God unless he is born again" (John 3:3). He might have said—"Heaven is a place for people with the Spirit, and you don't have what it takes."

Authentic biblical spirituality requires power. True spiritual power is a function of the presence of the Spirit. He is the source of spiritual empowerment.

There is another power shortage evident in the world today. Never before in American history have so many claimed to believe in Christ while having so little impact on their culture. Something is obviously wrong. Once upon a time in the United States, on any given Sunday, 43 percent of the population attended church. According to the Gallup poll, over 67 percent profess belief in Jesus as the Son of God. These are remarkable statistics. Yet 200 million professing Christians seem to have less impact on America than a small handful of men and women had on the world nearly two centuries ago. What is the problem? Could it be a massive power shortage?

"If you're not part of the solution, you're part of the problem." I'm not sure who first said it. Probably Eve to Adam. When we look at the spiritual condition of the world today we need to ask ourselves on which side of the equation we stand. What is the need of the hour? I would suggest it is a need for power. Without power the world will continue to head rapidly toward chaos and destruction.

Men and women of the Spirit. That's what we need. Men and women empowered and operating out of the dynamic of the promise and reality of that which Christ promised in the upper room and delivered on the day of Pentecost.

How can you be a man or woman of the Spirit? In the following chapters I hope to give you some tips. It is not as difficult or complex as it often seems. If you read carefully and prayerfully, and then faithfully attempt to do the assignments at the end of each chapter, you can become a man or woman of the Spirit.

—*Bob Beltz*
Castle Pines, Colorado 2025

CHAPTER ONE

UNDERSTANDING THE SPIRIT

"I will ask the Father, and He will give you
another Helper . . . the Spirit of truth."
—John 14:16-17

WHAT A LOUSY DAY!

John woke up on the proverbial wrong side of the bed. At breakfast he spilled coffee down the front of his favorite tie. Before he was out the door he had yelled at his wife, alienated his teenage daughter, and kicked the dog. On the drive to work he hollered borderline obscenities at any driver who was either going too slow in front of him or speeding past and then shifting into his lane.

Upon entering the door at work, the first person he saw was the last he wanted to see. Feldman was bound to complain about something, and John wasn't in the mood for it. Taking a quick turn, he headed in the other direction and worked his way around the building to his office. No sooner had he sat down at his desk than he realized his secretary had not provided him the one document he needed in order to finish his morning preparation.

At this point John put his head on the desk and began to pound with both fists. *How in the world am I ever going to deliver this morning's sermon?*

THE IMPOSSIBLE CHALLENGE

"Life is difficult." This observation constitutes the opening sentence of M. Scott Peck's best-selling book, *The Road Less Traveled.* "Life is complex." This further observation comes in the opening words of Peck's sequel, *Further Along the Road Less Traveled.* Let me take these observations one step further: "Life is impossible." This statement is always true when we view life from the perspective of a man or woman who desires to be the kind of person God wants them to be.

"Be perfect," Jesus instructed.

"I can't," the honest person replies.

This is the dilemma of the spiritual man or woman living in a fallen world. You and I don't have the ability to live the way God intended us to live. That is, not under our own power. We need help. We need a helper.

One night, Jesus met with twelve very ordinary men in an upper room in Jerusalem. They gathered there to share together the Passover meal. This meal pointed back to the great deliverance of the nation of Israel from its four hundred years of slavery in Egypt. On that first Passover night, God executed judgment on the Egyptians by putting to death the first-born male of every household where the blood of a lamb had not been applied to the doorposts and lintel of the home. From the palace of Pharaoh to the home of the lowest slave, cries rang out in Egypt as the Angel of Death moved across the land.

But wherever, in faith, the blood of a lamb had been applied, the angel passed over that house. This tenth plague freed the Israelites. When the people reached Mt. Sinai, God instructed them to remember this event every year by sharing together the Passover meal. This was the meal Jesus shared with His disciples that night in the upper room.

This was to be the final time Jesus would spend with the disciples before He went to the cross. This group of men had been together with Jesus for a little over three years. During that time they had seen Him do miracles, raise the dead, confront the Pharisees, and teach multitudes the message of God's kingdom.

I have always imagined that as they gathered in that room, Jesus would want to remind them of the most important lessons He had imparted over their years together. These were to be final instructions, the things that would be going through their minds as they watched Him hang from the cross.

The most comprehensive account of the Upper Room events is recorded for us in the gospel of John. It begins in the thirteenth chapter, where we are told that Jesus rose from the meal, wrapped a towel around His waist, and began to wash the disciples' feet. This was usually the job of the lowest slave in the household and a task that none of the disciples would have lowered themselves to perform. Peter protests; Jesus proceeds. When finished, Jesus told the disciples that He had set an example for them. They were to serve one another in the same way He had just served them.

Remember that only days earlier, this group was still arguing about who was the greatest of the bunch! But here Jesus redefined greatness in the terms of servanthood. Then, shortly after this demonstration of what He expected of the group, He gave them what He called "a new command" (John 13:34). He told them that the guiding rule of their lives was to have a love for one another that equaled His love for them. Unconditional love was to be the defining mark of a follower of Christ. If these twelve ordinary men took these two pieces of instruction seriously—servanthood and unconditional love—they should have been thinking, "This is impossible!"

THE HELPER IS HERE!

By nature, we are self-centered and selfish. Normally we don't want to serve; we want to *be* served. We want to be loved like Jesus loved, but we don't want to love others in the same way. The few who try discover quickly that they don't have the ability to do it.

The word *love* in the John 13 text is the Greek word *agape*. By definition, this is the love of God that is supernatural. It is a love we only become capable of expressing after we have had an enabling experience from God. That is why I think the sequence of Jesus' teaching is so important.

To add to the dilemma of the disciples, Jesus told them that He was going away. I can imagine the disciples looking around the room at each other and sending the nonverbal message, "Wait a minute! First He tells us to do the impossible, and then He tells us He won't even be here to help us when we fail!" It had to be discouraging, until Jesus told them about the Helper.

Jesus explained to these twelve men that it was actually to their advantage that He went away. He explained that with His departure He was going to send someone to help them—a paraclete. The word in Greek, *parakletos*, can be translated in a number of ways. It can mean "counselor," both in the sense of someone who is there to listen to you and be with you, and in the technical sense of "lawyer" or "advocate." Many modern translations use the word "helper." So basically, a paraclete is one who argues your case for you, one who comes alongside and helps you carry your load.

Jesus went on to tell these twelve men who their helper would be. In this chapter and those following, Jesus identified the helper as the Holy Spirit. He explained that the advantage of His imminent departure was that when He left, the Spirit would come. In order to understand why this would be more advantageous than having Jesus physically present, we need to understand a few facts about the Holy Spirit.

The Person of the Holy Spirit

Several years ago, I attended a bizarre meeting held at a retreat center in the Colorado mountains. Two groups had been invited to spend a weekend together. The purpose of the gathering was to see if any bridges of understanding could be erected to overcome any hostility between the two. The first group was comprised of a number of well-known leaders from the Evangelical Christian community. I tagged along with a friend who belonged to this group. The second group included a diverse group of leaders in what was known as the New Age movement.

If you landed at this retreat from another planet and were equipped with basic English language skills, at first blush you might have wondered what the problem was. Both groups used many of the same words to articulate their positions. You would have heard many references to Christ and an amazing amount of talk about "the spirit." It would have taken you several days to understand that these words carried significantly different content for the two groups.

The New Age group spoke of Christ as a cosmic spiritual power who descended at will upon certain earthlings for short periods of time and then moved on to its next subject. To the New Age group, the man Jesus just happened to be one of the lucky recipients of this honor. I had the sense that several members of the group were vying for the honor of being identified as the present incarnation of this cosmic "Christ."

There is actually nothing new about this New Age belief. It is at least as old as the second-century teachings of the Gnostics, who wreaked theological havoc upon the early church. These problems led second and third-century church leaders to formulate several of the early creeds. These statements of faith re-articulated the biblical position that Jesus was *the* Christ, the God-man, and that no division existed between Jesus and the Christ.

It soon became obvious to me that to the New Age group the "spirit" was some kind of a cosmic energy force. "Spirit" was impersonal. You could possess more or less of this force, and of course, it was always with you. Listening to their explanations gave me the sensation of entering a theological "Twilight Zone" or of becoming an extra on the set of *Star Wars*.

But the Holy Spirit is not a force. He is a person. He is a *he*, not an *it*. Jesus told the disciples, "I will ask the Father, and he will give you another Counselor, to be with you forever—the Spirit of truth. The world cannot accept *him*, because it neither sees *him* nor knows *him*. You know *him*, for *he* dwells with you and will be in you" (John 14:16-17, italics added for emphasis).

Consistently throughout the New Testament, the Holy Spirit is referred to with masculine personal pronouns. The neuter "it" is never used. In these days of gender insanity, the significance of the pronoun is not so much to be found in its gender. The primary significance is in the pronoun being *personal*.

His Personality

The Holy Spirit is a person who possesses all the dimensions of personality. What constitutes personality? Most psychologists would point to three qualities—intellect, emotion, and volition. Intellect is a function of personality. It must be present for personality to exist. An impersonal force does not have intellect. The Bible says that the Holy Spirit *knows* the mind of God (1 Corinthians 2:11). He possesses intellect.

Along with intellect, emotion is a function of personality. An impersonal force does not possess emotion. A force cannot feel, but the Holy Spirit does! In his letter to the believers in the city of Ephesus in Asia Minor, the apostle Paul cautioned them not to grieve the Spirit (Ephesians 4:30). It is possible to inflict emotional pain upon the Holy Spirit because He possesses emotion.

One final dimension of personality is volition—the ability to make choices and take action. A head of lettuce has no will, neither does an electrical charge, nor the "spirit" of the new agers. But the Holy Spirit possesses will. In his letter to the church in Corinth, Paul devotes a lengthy section to a discussion of the dynamics of spiritual gifts. He describes the origin of the diversity of the gifts by pointing out that it is the Holy Spirit who gives the gifts, distributing them to every believer "just as he wills" (1 Corinthians 12:11).

The Holy Spirit possesses intellect, emotion, and volition. He possesses these things because He is a person, not an impersonal force. Yet the Spirit is certainly unlike most people we know. He is a spirit person. We can't see Him, although He has the ability to manifest Himself in very tangible ways. At Jesus' baptism, He descended in the form of a dove. On the day of Pentecost, He showed up as tongues of fire. And even though He is not a force, He certainly has the ability to exert force.

This first truth about the Holy Spirit—His personhood—is extremely important. Whatever words we use to describe our experience with Him, we are always talking about dimensions of *a relationship with a person*. It is possible to become a modern gnostic, even as a Christian, when we think of the Spirit in terms of force or entity rather than person.

His Deity

The second truth the Bible teaches us about the person of the Holy Spirit is that He is God. As biblically based people of faith, we affirm the truth of God as "Trinity." By this word, we are attempting to summarize the biblical teaching that God is one being who exists in three persons: Father, Son, and Holy Spirit.

There is one true God. He has always been and will always be. He is the I AM. From eternity past through eternity future He existed as a tri-unity. He is three-in-one. I believe this is one of the most difficult concepts to understand in all of biblical theology. I recently read an observation that anyone who spends more than five minutes attempting to explain the Trinity has probably fallen into heresy! Certain metaphors can help us, but they usually fall short.

A vivid illustration of the Trinity concept came to me when my son and I were helping with a Thanksgiving outreach at our church. Our job was to pack each gift box with a bag of five potatoes. As we were grabbing potatoes and putting them in plastic bags, my son, Baker, said, "Look at this, Dad!" He had grabbed one of the most unique potatoes I had ever seen. It was one potato, no question about it, but it was definitely made up of three distinct potatoes that had somehow grown together. You could see the form of all three individual potatoes, but there was a point where the three merged together into one where you couldn't find any sign of distinction.

I kept that crazy potato in my office until it rotted. I even tried to figure out how to perform taxidermy on it. Although imperfect, it seemed like a great model of the Trinity. God is one God, but He exists as three persons. God is Father; God is Son; and God is Holy Spirit. Jesus was not just the Son of God, He was in fact God the Son.

In the same way, the Holy Spirit is not just the Spirit of God, He is God the Spirit. We have several good biblical passages that validate this truth.

In the early days of the apostolic ministry, two believers named Ananias and Sapphira made a big mistake. Some of the believers, like Barnabas, were selling all of their goods and making their resources available to struggling Christians in the city of Jerusalem. Ananias and Sapphira also sold a piece of property, but kept some of the proceeds for themselves while telling the church they had given everything. There is no indication that they had to give everything. The problem was in the lie they told.

When confronting them, Peter said they had lied to the Holy Spirit (Acts 5:4). The fact that someone could lie to the Spirit is another indication that the Spirit is a person. You can't lie to an impersonal force. But the main thrust of the passage in regards to the deity of the Spirit comes in the next verse where we read that Peter said, "You have not lied to men but to God," (verse 4). To lie to the Spirit is to lie to God. In other words, the Holy Spirit is God.

Throughout the Bible you will discover that many of the attributes of God are possessed by the Spirit. He is eternal (Hebrews 9:14), omnipotent (Luke 1:35-

37), omnipresent (Psalm 139:7), and omniscient (1 Corinthians 2:11). All that is true of God the Father and God the Son, is true of God the Spirit.

WHAT THE SPIRIT DOES

The second main category concerning the Holy Spirit, after we've explored who He is, has to do with discovering what He does. We could begin by saying that the Holy Spirit does everything that God does. In every act of God, from creation to redemption, through the creation of the new heavens and new earth, the Holy Spirit is present and active. Because of the nature of God, He has to be. Father, Son, and Holy Spirit always exist and act together.

In my book *Daily Disciplines for the Christian Man*, I introduced a concept I call the interpenetration of the personalities of the Godhead. In the book I used the classic diagram of three circles intersecting each other to illustrate this concept (see figure 1.1).

In some ways this looks a great deal like my three-in-one potato. Notice that there is a point at which all three circles intersect. There is within each of the circles a point where the other two circles are present. This is what interpenetration means.

Figure 1.1: The Tri-unity

In regard to God, interpenetration means that wherever one member of the Trinity is present, the other two are also present. This is why Jesus could say to Philip, "Anyone who has seen me has seen the Father" (John 14:9). Jesus goes on to say, "Don't you believe that I am in the Father, and that the Father is in me?" (verse 10). To see Jesus was not just to see what the Father was like. To see Jesus was to actually see the Father because He and the Father are one (John 10:30). Their personalities interpenetrate.

In the same way, the Holy Spirit is always present wherever the Father or the Son is present. He is always active wherever the Father and the Son are active. Because of this, every act of God is the work of the Spirit.

But the Spirit plays a special role in relationship to the work of God in the life of the believer. His work can be broken down into four main categories.

Category #1—Preparation

Many of us remember the days before we gave our lives to Jesus. If you were like me, you had two big problems: a hard heart and a closed mind. I remember friends telling me about Christ, but at the time it all sounded as if they were speaking a foreign language. I didn't get it. I had a hard heart and a closed mind. Years of living in rebellion against God, and indifference toward the spiritual life, had taken its toll. Had something not changed, I would never have been able to see the truth about Jesus or respond to Him.

Something did happen. The Holy Spirit began to work on me. He used people and circumstances to "soften me up." I began to sense my need and to have a new openness to thinking about God. People were praying for me, and the Spirit was working.

The Holy Spirit also orchestrates circumstances to draw us to Christ. The classic example comes in the book of Acts when the Spirit led Philip into an encounter with a man from Ethiopia (Acts 8:26-40). The Ethiopian's heart was already softened, his mind open. He had gone up to Jerusalem to worship God and was on his way home.

Having stopped along the road, the Ethiopian was reading the Bible in his chariot when the Spirit instructed Philip to go up to the chariot and talk to the man. Just as Philip arrived, the Ethiopian was reading from Isaiah 53, one of the great messianic prophecies. Talk about orchestration! He asked Philip who the prophet was talking about, and Philip told him about Jesus.

In our own lives, the orchestration might not have been quite so dramatic, but I'm sure if you think carefully, you could recall times in which the Spirit was at work. In my life, I think of one humorous situation I am convinced the Spirit used in my journey.

Before my conversion, I was a tough nut to crack. In the early days of my exposure to Jesus, I was extremely resistant. Then, when I began to respond to the "softening" process, I felt as though I was too far gone to be a Christian. One Saturday during this time, I was invited to play touch football with a team sponsored by a church that many of my old friends had started attending. We were playing another church team, and right in the middle of the game a big fight broke out. I remember standing there, as an unbeliever, watching all these Christians rolling around on the ground, fighting with each other. It might seem strange, but the first thought that came to my mind was, "I think I could be a Christian!"

I'm not saying that the Holy Spirit orchestrated the fight. I'm sure a great deal of confession and reconciliation happened after the game. But I do believe He orchestrated my being there to see the "human side" of the Christian life. He also used this event to lead me to the next step.

In the process of preparation, the Holy Spirit creates within us a sense of our need. Jesus told the disciples that the Spirit would "convict the world in regard to sin" (John 16:8). As our hearts soften and our minds open, we begin to understand that we have a big problem. We might get honest about the fact that something is missing in our lives, and that it might be God. When we reach this point, we may also begin to sense that if God is the answer, then we have an even bigger problem. We might not be able to call it sin, but we know what it is. Something is wrong with the way we have lived. Conviction is at work. This is the work of the Spirit.

The final work of the Spirit in the process of preparation is the bringing of clarity. Suddenly all comes clear. We see that God loves us, but that our sin has separated us from Him. We see clearly that Jesus is the answer to our dilemma. We understand that we have to make a choice. We know! That is the work of clarity; the light bulb flashes on.

Category #2—Regeneration

In the next chapter we are going to look in detail at the process theologians call regeneration. The term refers to the experience of spiritual birth. It occurs when clarity leads to a decision to embrace Jesus Christ as Lord and Savior.

I am convinced, through the Bible and through my personal experience, that the ability to even approach that decision is a work of the Holy Spirit. When I open my life to Jesus and invite Him to come into my life, He comes. But how does He come to me? He sends His Spirit.

The Holy Spirit is the agent of the new birth. When He comes to invade my life, I am born spiritually, and Jesus Christ dwells within me. Wherever the Spirit is present, Jesus is present.

Category #3—Transformation

The Holy Spirit is the change agent in the life of the believer. From the moment of new birth, the Spirit begins to change us from the inside out. This process of change is referred to in the Bible as *sanctification*.

This word is the translation of the Greek *hagiodzo*. It is one of the words in the *hagios* family that has a relationship to the concept of being holy. The word *hagios*, translated "holy," means "dedicated" or "set apart for God's purposes." God wants to make us holy men and women, set apart for God's plans and purposes. In order for this to be fully accomplished we need to be transformed. When we come to Christ out of a background in the fallen world, we usually bring with us quite a bit of baggage. We are damaged emotionally, confused mentally, distorted ethically, and twisted morally. In other words, we are *un-*holy. Our lives are major reclamation projects. This is the miracle of sanctification. God has planned to change us so that we can become conformed to the image of Christ (Romans 8:29-30).

How do we become holy? We will cover many facets of the answer to this question in coming chapters, but for now let me just say the Holy Spirit makes us holy. He is the *Holy* Spirit (same word, *hagios*, in Greek). He begins to work in our inner person to heal damaged emotions. He uses our interface with the Bible to renew our confused minds. He works in our value systems to create a new set of ethics. He empowers us to overcome the habits of the old nature and begins to produce spiritual fruit through us.

We can act religious, but that is not authentic change. Religiosity is simply external conformity to some imagined definition of spirituality or goodness. Authentic change takes place from the inside out. All authentic transformation is the work of the Holy Spirit.

Category #4—Activation

The final category of the work of the Spirit has to do with how the Holy Spirit empowers and equips us to fulfill our role in God's kingdom. The Spirit is the power source of the Christian life. Jesus told the disciples they had a world-changing task to accomplish. "Go into all the world," He commissioned (Mark 16:15). But He cautioned them not to attempt to go until they had received the power to accomplish the job. He said, "Stay in the city until you have been clothed with power from on high" (Luke 24:49). Jesus was speaking of the coming of the Spirit. The Spirit, who had been "with" them, was now going to be "in" them. His indwelling would be an empowering event—"You will receive power when the Holy Spirit comes upon you" (Acts 1:8). The job the Christian has to do requires supernatural enabling. This enabling is the work of the Spirit. Learning to tap into His power is the difference between an effective and productive spiritual experience and a dry, dull religiosity.

Along with imparting power, the Holy Spirit also endows us with gifts, special abilities that we can use to accomplish our part in God's plans. Every person in whom the Spirit has come to dwell has been given one or more of these *charismata*. As we have already seen, which gifts the person receives is a choice of the Spirit (1 Corinthians 12:11). We will explore the gifts, and how to discover yours, in chapter 6 of this book.

Preparation, regeneration, transformation, and activation. All four are the work of the Spirit. He is the experiential link in the plans of God, for your life and mine. I hope you can begin to see how futile it would be to try to live the Christian life without a solid understanding and experience of the Holy Spirit. It would be like trying to drive your car without turning on the ignition. You could keep pushing the gas pedal and turning the steering wheel until you were exhausted, but you wouldn't get very far. Unfortunately, that is what far too many people in the church are trying to do. They haven't learned how to be men and women of the Spirit. Fortunately, you are not going to be one of them.

ASSIGNMENT: CHAPTER ONE

Personal Application

1. Read John 14 daily this week. Underline every reference to the Holy Spirit.
2. Try to write a definition that answers the question: "What is the Holy Spirit?"
3. Pray daily that the Holy Spirit will help you understand and know Him better.

Group Discussion

1. What was your life like before Christ? Talk about some of your attitudes and viewpoints. What things were most important to you then?
2. When did the Holy Spirit first begin to soften you? To what extent did you realize that you were being "prepared" for something new?
3. Who were the most influential people in your "softening up" process? What things did these people do or say to make a difference? Could you emulate any of these behaviors with others?
4. How radical has the change process of sanctification been in your life? Name some of the "old ways" that have been difficult for you to give up. Name some of the major changes you've experienced.

5.   What evidence have you seen in one another that the gifts of the Spirit are at work among you (in your small group or in your church congregation)?

6.   What questions do you still have about the Holy Spirit and His ministry?

7.   What step(s) could you take this week to become more open to the Spirit's wisdom, power, and guidance?

CHAPTER TWO

BORN OF THE SPIRIT

"Don't marvel that I said to you,
"You must be born again."
—John 3:7

IT WAS ONE OF THOSE CALLS a pastor dreads. John and Renee were phoning from Littleton Hospital. Something had gone wrong with the pregnancy, and the doctors had advised them to contact their pastor. Nine months of joy and expectation were turning into heartbreak and anguish.

By the time I reached the hospital the baby had been delivered—stillborn. The cord had wrapped around the baby's neck in the womb, cutting off life-giving oxygen. By the time a fetal monitor was in place, it was already too late. Renee had gone through labor only to deliver a lifeless baby. She and John were devastated.

We hugged and cried, and then John did a remarkable thing. He went to Renee's side and lifted a small bundle wrapped in a hospital blanket. Then he brought it over to me. I reached out, cradled the lifeless form in my arms, and cried. I kept thinking, *It isn't supposed to be like this.*

Born dead—a complete contradiction of terms. It isn't supposed to be like this. John and Renee's story has a happy ending though. A year later a new baby sprang from the womb, full of life and vitality. I remember the first time I saw the young couple holding their little newborn. What a contrast between the joy of life and the grief of death! The comparison led me to wonder if this is how God looks at His children.

A VERY RELIGIOUS MAN

The Bible tells us that we are born dead. "You were dead in your transgressions and sins," the Apostle Paul wrote to the believers in Ephesus (Ephesians 2:1). Every person on the face of the planet comes into the world alive physically, but dead spiritually. As the Father looks at His lifeless children, He longs for one thing—that they might come alive. He is the God who imparts life. This truth was at the heart of the message Jesus delivered to an exemplary religious leader of the Jews named Nicodemus. The encounter unfolds in the third chapter of the gospel

of John, as Nicodemus comes at night to talk with Jesus
in a quiet, undisturbed way about the great issues of life.

We are told of three religious credentials Nicodemus
brought to this meeting. First, Nicodemus was a Pharisee,
an important fact when we understand the issue Jesus
addressed with him. The Pharisees were the religious
leaders of the vast majority of the Jews living in Israel
at the time of Christ. The sect was committed to a strict
observance of the Law of Moses and the oral tradition of
former rabbis. The word *Pharisee* comes from a Hebrew
word, *perushim*, which means "the separated ones."

A Little History

Phariseeism developed in the intertestamental
period; the four hundred years between the end of the
Old Testament and the beginning of the New Testament.
If you read through the entire Old Testament, you won't
find one Pharisee; however, when you begin to read the
New Testament, you find the Pharisees playing a central
role in the life of Israel.

The Pharisees were a group that developed out of
the lessons learned in Israel's defeat and captivity in
Babylon during the period of the kings. The constant
tendency of the Jewish people was to drift into idolatry
and immorality as they embraced the religious and social

practices of their Canaanite neighbors. God sent prophets to warn the people that if they didn't change their ways and turn back to a sincere faith in God, He would send disaster upon them.

The northern kingdom of Israel existed from about 930 BC until 722 BC. During these years the northern kingdom had nineteen kings. They all led the people away from the Lord and into idolatry. As a result, in 722 BC, the Assyrian Empire conquered Israel. Through the philosophy of conquest practiced by the Assyrians, they effectively destroyed the identity of the ten northern tribes.

During these years the southern kingdom of Judah had a number of kings that led the nation in repentance and a return to their spiritual roots. Unfortunately, eventually, they too reached a point where they became subject to God's judgment. In 586 BC, the Babylonian Empire destroyed the city of Jerusalem and took captive the leaders of the people. This captivity lasted for seventy years.

When the people returned to rebuild the temple and the walls of the city, they had learned their lesson. A rigid spirit of legalistic adherence to the Law and to monotheism took hold. The Pharisees were born out of this desire to do everything "just right" from now on. It is safe to say they represented the most religious segment of the Jewish population. They memorized the Torah. They prayed three times a day. They attended and led services at the synagogue, and they tithed religiously (excuse the pun). Nicodemus was a Pharisee.

The second credential of Nicodemus we see in this passage is the fact that he was a member of the Jewish ruling class. The Greek text simply says, "a ruler of the Jews." This most likely means that Nicodemus was a member of the Sanhedrin. The Sanhedrin was the most powerful group of men in Israel. It has been compared to the Supreme Court, but that comparison doesn't really do it justice (excuse another pun!). We need to remember that the religious and civil distinctions we know in our culture were not the norm in Israel. The Law of Moses was the law—both religious and civil. Every facet of Jewish life was governed by it. The Sanhedrin was the final authority in all matters relating to the Law, for every Jew in the world. The Sanhedrin was composed of seventy members. Nicodemus was one of these men.

Nicodemus's third credential comes in a reference Jesus makes to him as "the teacher of Israel." The presence of the definite article "the" in the Greek text indicates that Nicodemus held a unique position among the rabbis of Jerusalem.

If you put all these credentials together you get a picture of an extremely religious man. You might even think of Nicodemus as a model of the most religious man possible. This makes his dilemma all the more significant.

The New Birth

Nicodemus had recognized that something was different about Jesus. He makes this known by addressing Jesus as "a teacher who has come from God." My sense is that Nicodemus was distinguishing Jesus from all those rabbis, like himself, who taught with human credentials but without spiritual power. Nicodemus said to Jesus, "No one could perform the signs you are doing if God were not with him" (John 3:2).

So Nicodemus came to Jesus with a statement, but Jesus cut straight to the question in this man's heart by responding with a solemn declaration: "Truly, truly, I say to you, unless one is born again, he is not able to see the kingdom of God" (John 3:3).

But Nicodemus wanted to know with certainty what being born again was all about. You almost sense his uncertainty in the encounter. Jesus gave him the answer in verse 5: "Truly, truly, I say to you, unless one is born of water and spirit he cannot enter the kingdom of God."

In the Greek text, Jesus begins by using the formula *amen* and *amen*. Like early versions of the Bible, I have translated this phrase, "Truly, truly." The force of the expression in the original language is to let the hearer know that the speaker is making a statement that carries absolute certainty.

"This is absolutely true!" is how Jesus began His response.

The expression "born again" has received a great deal of press in recent years. Unfortunately, outside the Christian community it is usually viewed in a negative manner. It has become a cultural cliché for narrow-mindedness and fundamentalistic rigidity. This is tragic. The phrase denotes a critically important reality. The word we usually translate "again" is the Greek word *anothen*. It has three shades of meaning. It does mean "again" in the sense of "a second time." In this case, Jesus is informing Nicodemus that he needs a second birth. But *anothen* also carries the sense of again as in "that which is *qualitatively different* from that which came before." To be born again means having a birth of a different kind from the first birth. Finally, the word speaks of that which is "from above." This is perhaps the most important dimension of what Jesus is saying. He is telling Nicodemus that the birth he needs in order to enter the kingdom of God must come from above.

If this seems a bit confusing to you, take heart! Nicodemus didn't understand, either. "How can this be?" he asked Jesus. In response, Jesus explained the essence of the human condition. When we understand what Jesus taught here, we will have a greater appreciation for the ministry of the Holy Spirit in our lives.

Jesus spoke to Nicodemus of the difference between physical birth and spiritual birth. He said, "That which is born of the flesh is flesh, but the Spirit gives birth to spirit" (verse 6). Every person living on the planet begins life with physical birth. But, from the moment of physical birth, every person on the planet has a huge problem— spiritual death.

To understand what Jesus is saying, it would be helpful to go back to the book of Genesis and see what was going on "in the beginning." The second chapter of Genesis gives us a thumbnail sketch of the way God designed life to be. At the heart of this description, we find a statement regarding the three dimensions of life God intended all men and women to possess.

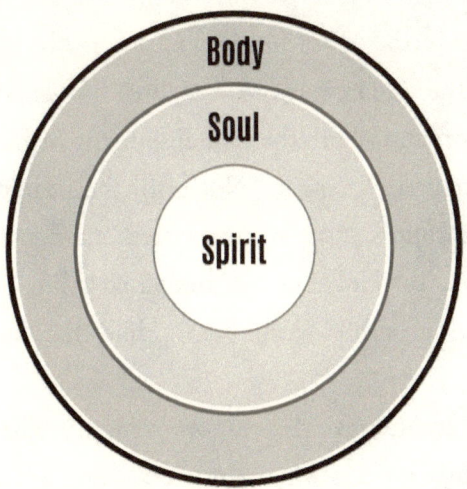

Figure 2.1: Three-Dimensional Man

The seventh verse of the second chapter reveals that God fashioned man from the dust of the earth, breathed into him the breath of life, and man became a living being. In this verse we see the physical, emotional, and spiritual components of what it meant to be a human being, created in the image of God. (see Figure 2.1) The outer circle represents our physical being. Like a skilled craftsman, God formed Adam from the dust of the earth. There is even a play on words between the name Adam and the Hebrew word for earth—*adamah*.

Into this physical being God breathed the breath of life. This is where this text gives us critical insight into the nature of humanity. There are two words used in this statement that need further exploration if we're to grasp the significance of what God does at this point. The first is the word *breath*. God breathes life into Adam. The Hebrew word for breath—*nashemah*—is used synonymously in the Old Testament with the word *ruach*—translated "spirit." Not until the time of Christ does the significance of this statement come to full expression. The Holy Spirit is the source of life. Jesus says, "The Spirit gives life" (John 6:63). Hold that thought for a minute.

The second word in the sentence that needs some explanation is *life*. In this text the Hebrew word translated "life" is *chaiyim*. If you have ever seen the play *Fiddler on the Roof*, you probably remember Tevye, the main character, singing the words, "To life, to life, *l'chaiyim!*" The interesting characteristic of this word is that it appears in its plural form. The *im* ending in Hebrew makes a word plural. Although this ending can carry other significance than plurality, we definitely have a hint of more than one kind of life here.

Again, it is not until the New Testament teaching of Christ that the plurality of life becomes clear. In the New Testament there are actually two different words used for, and translated as, our word *life*. The Greek word *psuche* is often used to communicate the concept of physical life, while the word *zoe* is used to speak of spiritual life.

A good example of this distinction is found in the tenth chapter of John, where Jesus is speaking about His role as the Good Shepherd. He declares, "I have come that they may have life, and have it more abundantly" (John 10:10). Here, the word *zoe* appears in the Greek text. Jesus is saying, "I have come to give you spiritual life." In the next sentence He explains how He will give life. He says, "The good shepherd lays down his life for the sheep" (verse 11). Here the word *psuche* appears. Jesus is telling the disciples that He is going to lay down His physical life in order that they might have spiritual life. Now, let's go back to Genesis.

God breathes His Spirit into Adam, and Adam becomes a living being, or soul. The Hebrew word *nephesh* can have either meaning. Humans become three-dimensional and possess two distinct kinds of life—physical and spiritual. We could illustrate this reality with Figure 2.2.

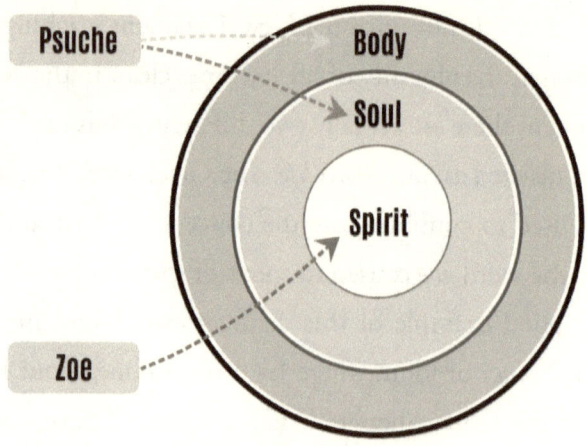

Figure 2.2: Spiritual Life

The three circles represent the three dimensions within which we were designed to operate. At the core we were intended to be spiritual men and women, possessing the very Spirit of God, who is the source of *zoe* life. Tragically, something went wrong. God placed Adam in a utopian environment and provided for all his needs. He also made Adam a free moral agent, having the ability to make choices and decisions. The most important decision had to do with Adam's relationship with God. In this realm, God gave one restriction to Adam in Eden: "Don't eat from the Tree of the Knowledge of Good and Evil." I promise, it wasn't an apple—or sex!

This tree gave Adam the opportunity to make the most important decision he would ever make. To obey was to let God be God. To disobey would constitute a rejection of God and the choice to act as his own god. This choice was to have grave consequences.

God's prohibition carried with it a warning. If Adam chose to eat the forbidden fruit, he would suffer death. God said, "In the day you eat of it you will surely die" (Genesis 2:17).

Again, there is an important nuance in how God said this. If we translated this statement out of the Hebrew with a wooden literalism it would read, "Dying, you will die." Although this grammatical structure is normally intended to add emphasis, there is surely a hint here of two kinds of death.

This becomes clearer when we see what happens in Genesis 3 and 4. Genesis 3 records the tragic choices of Adam and Eve as the tempter convinces them they will not die. They both eat the forbidden fruit. Immediately the consequences of their decision become apparent.

Spiritual Death

The first observation we can make is that they did not fall down dead—yet. Physical death did not occur immediately, but something else had happened. Immediately, we find Adam hiding from God. He was afraid. Compare this to the relationship that existed in Genesis 2 and you can see something has gone wrong. When confronted by God about his action, Adam rationalized that the woman God gave him was responsible. Blame, projection, and rationalization are well-known defense mechanisms of a damaged emotional system.

What has happened? Adam and Eve have died spiritually. Death is the absence of life. What is the source of spiritual life? The Holy Spirit. What happens when the Holy Spirit no longer dwells within the human spirit? Death. "The wages of sin is death," (Romans 6:23). Spiritual death causes a separation between humanity and God. Fellowship is broken and the relationship is seriously impaired. Nothing is as it was intended to be.

It was as if God were saying to Adam, "I have given you life by sending my Spirit to dwell in your spirit. I am present within you because the Spirit is God. Wherever He is present, I am present. I can only reside where I am allowed to be who I am—God. If you choose to be god, I will leave—I will withdraw my Spirit. When that happens, you will be without spiritual life—you will die spiritually—and eventually, because you have lost my life, you will die physically."

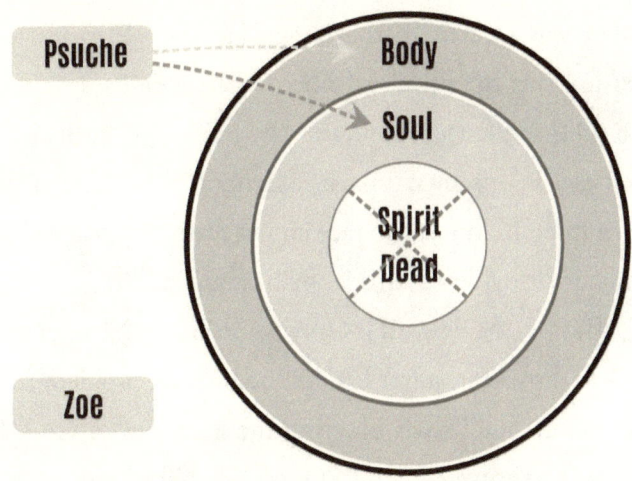

Figure 2.3: Spiritual Death

At the core of our being, the spirit is now dead. This can be illustrated by Figure 2.3. The emotional system that was designed to be under the dominant influence of the Spirit is now without that influence. The body, designed to be the servant of the Spirit and the psyche, becomes the dominant influence—thus giving fallen humanity the nomenclature of "flesh."

Genesis 4 introduces us to the first instance of physical death. Adam and Eve stand over the dead body of their son Abel. We can hardly imagine what must have been going through their minds as they realized, "This is death!"

Chapter 5 of Genesis begins by reminding us that Adam was created in the image of God. Then, as the text gives us the details of Adam's descendants, it makes the subtle shift to the phrase, "he had a son in his own likeness, in his own image" (Genesis 5:3). Flesh gave birth to flesh. The entire race comes forth physically alive but spiritually dead. This is the human condition.

This is the lesson Jesus was teaching Nicodemus. This nighttime inquirer had a fundamental problem that would keep him from entering the kingdom of God. It was as if Jesus were saying, "Good job, Nick. You are one heck of a guy. You keep the Law as best you can. You study your Bible and teach at the synagogue. You tithe all your income and render just and fair judgments in the Sanhedrin. You pray and go to worship. You do all kinds of good things. You have only one problem: You are dead! And if something doesn't happen to you to change that fact, you will never enter the kingdom of heaven."

LIFE MADE POSSIBLE AGAIN

Nicodemus needed a new birth. He needed the dead part in him to come alive. That which was true of

Nicodemus is true of every man and woman born on planet Earth. We are a race born dead, a tragedy that would keep us out of God's kingdom were it not for the fact that God has done something to make it possible to have a new kind of birth.

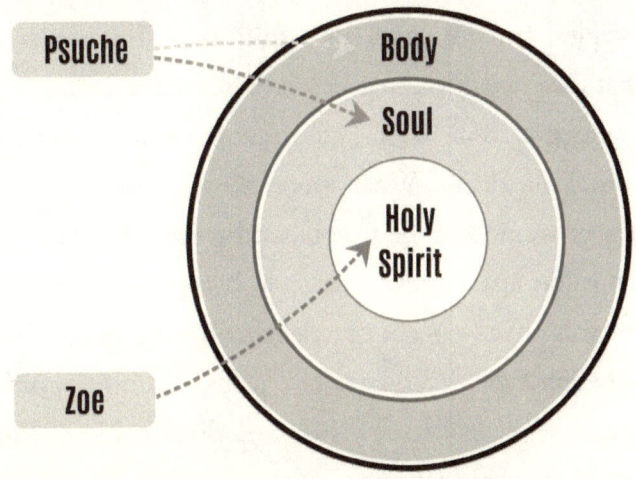

Figure 2.4: Spiritual Birth

Jesus said, "I have come that they may have life *[zoe]* " (John 10:10). "I am the way and the truth and the life *[zoe]*" (John 14:6). "In him was life *[zoe]* " (John 1:4). Jesus is a life-giver. He is the source of *zoe*. He makes it possible for people to experience a spiritual birth. This birth is a function of what He accomplished on the cross and what happens to us when we invite Him into our lives as Lord and Savior.

When we open our lives to Jesus and invite Him to come in, He enters. He does this by means of the Holy Spirit. Remember, wherever the Spirit is present, Jesus is present. The Holy Spirit is the agent of the new birth. It is His very presence in our life that gives us life. It is as if God breathes on us again, as Jesus did with the disciples, and we come alive spiritually. This reality is what theologians call regeneration (see figure 2.4).

Regeneration is the beginning of all authentic biblical spirituality. When it occurs, we become spiritual men or women in the true biblical sense. That which is impossible apart from Christ, now becomes possible. We are positioned to begin experiencing the influence of the Holy Spirit over every area of our lives. In other words, we can be filled with the Spirit. We'll discover more about that in the next chapter.

ASSIGNMENT: CHAPTER TWO

Personal Application

1. Read the third chapter of John every day this week.
2. If you've asked Jesus into your life and experienced the new birth, give thanks to the Lord.
3. Spend some time every day this week in prayer, thanking God that He has given you the gift of life.

Group Discussion

1. What does the phrase "born again" mean to you? Compare and contrast the biblical meaning with what you think your neighbor understands about it. How does today's media portray it?
2. Imagine being Nicodemus. What things would give you confidence about the health of your spiritual life? What doubts might you have?
3. When have you been most aware of being spiritually alive? Spiritually dead?
4. Is being born again always a sudden event—or can it be a process over time? Share with each other about your born- again experience.
5. What aspects of Jesus' "technique" with Nicodemus show us how to effectively share our faith?
6. In what ways do you, personally, sense the presence of God's Spirit in your life? What things help you maintain this awareness during the day?

CHAPTER 3

FILLED WITH THE SPIRIT

"Be being filled with the Spirit."
—Ephesians 5:18

IT WAS A BEAUTIFUL SUMMER night in Kansas City. But this fact didn't change my sensation of having just shown up at a party from which everyone else was heading home. The room swirled in apparent chaos. People were shouting or moaning, looks of either indescribable ecstasy or unbearable pain on their faces. Others lined the front of the room, falling backward, one by one, into the arms of men who seemed to anticipate their sudden collapse. Still others were simply swaying in silence, arms lifted to heaven, tears running down their cheeks. I felt as though I was the only one not "getting it."

What made the experience even more confusing was the fact that I wanted to "get it"—whatever "it" was. I was a new Christian and I wanted to experience everything God had for my life. A friend had suggested I go to this meeting. When I arrived, the event was already in full swing. As I stood and watched in utter amazement, person after person approached and asked if I had "gotten it." My spiritual mentor tried to explain what was happening in that building on that particular summer evening. But fifty-five years later, I'm still not completely sure what I think about it.

"Be filled with the Spirit." This was the simple exhortation of the Apostle Paul to the believers in the city of Ephesus (Ephesians 5:18). It sits among at least fifty other brief instructions Paul gives these men and women in chapters 4 through 6 of the book of Ephesians. Apparently his immediate audience knew exactly what he meant and how to fulfill the mandate. Had he known how the phrase would be debated and distorted over the next twenty centuries, I'm sure he would have wanted to go into a bit more explanation.

WHAT'S THE MEANING?

What does it mean to be "filled" with the Spirit? This is a question every man or woman who seeks to live a spiritually-based life needs to know how to answer. By way of review, let me remind you that the Holy Spirit is a person. In the last chapter you came to understand that when you opened your life to Christ and invited Him to come in, you were indwelled by this Spirit person. He brought new life to you. In fact, it is His very presence in your life that is the source of spiritual regeneration. Once the Spirit has imparted life by His presence, you are living in a dynamic relationship with Him. His activity in your life is described by the use of a number of words in the Bible, but all these words are simply communicating different spiritual realities created by your relationship with the Spirit. In the early days of my spiritual life, I struggled with a faulty belief about this reality. I tended to conceptualize the Holy Spirit more as a force or substance than as a person. As a result, I tended to think of myself as having more or less of the Spirit. It was as if I saw my life as a glass that was either half full or half empty. I have discovered that many believers operate out of this false concept. If the Holy Spirit is a person, we can't have more or less of Him. We can have degrees of relationship, however. We can experience more or less of His influence in our lives.

I once heard a story about the famous evangelist D. L. Moody. Moody was the Billy Graham of his day.

Through his life, many thousands of men and women came to know Christ. As a result, he was in great demand as a speaker.

During Moody's time it was common for a number of churches in a city to work together to hold evangelistic meetings, not unlike the Promise Keepers rallies of our day. One time, a number of the leading ministers in Chicago met together to plan a series of city-wide meetings, and they had to decide who they would invite to speak at the campaign. Virtually everyone in the room wanted D. L. Moody.

Just as the group was making it a unanimous decision, one of the ministers—a somewhat arrogant young man—stood and addressed the others. He said, "D. L. Moody. D. L. Moody. Why does it have to be D. L. Moody? Does D. L. Moody have a monopoly on the Holy Spirit?"

The room grew quiet, and after a brief moment, another minister rose to address the group. This older gentleman, with a gracious spirit, spoke in a gentle voice in response, "No, D. L. Moody does not have a monopoly on the Holy Spirit. But the Holy Spirit has a monopoly on D. L. Moody."

This is a great illustration of what it means to be "filled" with the Spirit. It is a state of relationship with the Holy Spirit in which He has a monopoly on our lives and has freedom to do, in and through us, all that He pleases. This was the secret of D. L. Moody's effectiveness as an evangelist. By training he was a shoe salesman. But God took hold of his life and he learned to let the Spirit "fill" him.

The word we translate "filled" in Ephesians 5:18 is the Greek word *pleroo*. When used in the context of relationship it can mean "dominant influence." Notice the analogy Paul uses in the Ephesians passage. He tells his readers not to be drunk on wine, but rather to be filled with the Spirit. When a man or woman has had too much to drink, we refer to them as being "under the influence." A DUI violation is given when someone has been drinking and driving. In the same way that a person becomes dominantly influenced by drinking too much alcohol, a spiritual man or woman is to allow the indwelling Holy Spirit to be the dominant influence in their life. We are to be recognized as being LUI, that is, living under the influence—not of alcohol, but of the Holy Spirit.

One simple way to understand what this means is to think of your life as having a control center where someone always is in charge. The image of a throne has been used since the time of Teresa of Avila, who lived in the sixteenth century, to capture this concept. Your life might then be illustrated this way before Christ:

S - Self is on the throne
† - Christ is outside the life

Figure 3.1: Before Christ

At any given moment, this throne is occupied either by Christ or by self. Before the new birth experience, which we studied in the last chapter, self or ego always sat enthroned (see Figure 3:1). When we opened our life and asked Jesus to come in, He came and occupied this place. It could be argued that you can ask Jesus into your life and still have self in control, but this is a pretty strange understanding of the concept of repentance and also of who Jesus is.

Jesus is Lord. He is God. The essence of sin is wanting to be your own god, instead of letting God be God. Repentance is the recognition that that is exactly what you have been doing and that you desire to turn from that way of living. Because Jesus is both Lord and God, to ask Jesus into your life is to surrender the throne to Him. We will see in subsequent chapters that the struggle we face on a daily basis is to let Him continue to occupy that place, and not to usurp His lordship in our inner life. Conversion could be diagrammed like figure 3.2.

✝ - Christ is in the life and on the throne
S - Self is yielding to Christ

Figure 3.2: Christ Enthroned

Because Jesus dwells in us in the person of the Holy Spirit, we can understand Jesus on the throne as synonymous with being filled with the Spirit. He is in the driver's seat. He is the dominant source of influence. We are living our life in submission to Him. Now comes an interesting observation.

Keep On Being Filled

When we read Ephesians 5:18 in our English Bibles we can get the impression that Paul is speaking about a one-time experience. But when we go back to the original language of the New Testament and study this verse and its grammatical structure, we discover that the command has a different emphasis.

The verb tense of the word *pleroo* in this verse is the Greek present tense. The force of this tense implies ongoing, habitual action. If we were to translate the verse with a wooden literalism it would instruct us to "be being filled, continually, with the Holy Spirit." This is not a static command. It is an exhortation to an ongoing state of relationship in which we continually allow the Holy Spirit to control, empower, and influence our lives. At any given moment, one of two conditions characterizes our spiritual life. Either Jesus Christ is in control by means of the indwelling Holy Spirit, or our own self or ego is in control. We are living in one of these two realities (see Figure 3.3).

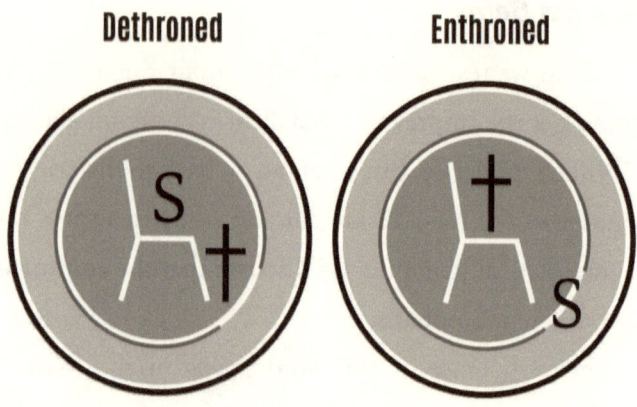

Figure 3.3: "Dethroned"/ "Enthroned"

To "be being" filled means that we maintain a consistent state of allowing the Holy Spirit to be the dominant influence in our lives. We keep Jesus enthroned.

How can I be sure this is my condition? Paul gives a few hints in this passage. Notice the behaviors that accompany this spiritual condition. Paul says that we will sing, give thanks, and live in a servant-based state of relationship when the Holy Spirit is in control (Ephesians 5:19-21).

As important as these outward effects might be, the true test of whether or not we are being filled with the Spirit is the way this reality is manifested in changed character over the years. Our lives will begin to generate new indicators of internal change. We will become spiritually productive as the Holy Spirit lives in and through us, bearing what the Bible calls the fruit of the Spirit. In the next chapter we'll spend some time learning more about this dimension of becoming a man or woman of the Spirit.

HOW TO BE FILLED WITH THE SPIRIT

I have attempted to demonstrate that biblically, being "filled with the Spirit" describes a quality of relationship with Jesus in which we are allowing His Spirit within us to be the dominant influence in and through our lives. How do we enter into this quality of relationship? Let me attempt to break the process down logically. The danger of doing this is that it might indicate a mechanical process instead of describing a dynamic relationship. I hope we can take the parts of the process and apply them in such a way that we will understand how to use them as tools to keep our relationship with Jesus Christ vital and dynamic.

I find it helpful to think things through, step-by-step. So consider these four "simple steps" to being filled with the Holy Spirit.

Step One: Desire

To be filled with the Spirit, you have to *want* to be filled with the Spirit. This may sound redundant, but in reality it is perhaps the most important element of the process. "What do you want me to do for you?" Jesus asked this question of a blind man who came to Him for healing (Mark 10:51). It might have seemed like a foolish question at the time. It actually was an extremely profound inquiry. Did the man really want to see? Or had he grown so comfortable in his blindness that he really didn't want a different kind of life at all? "I want to see," the blind man answered. Once the desire was affirmed, Jesus healed him.

What do you want? Do you want Jesus to be Lord over your life, and His Spirit to live in you to control, guide, and empower your life? Do you want to relinquish your own autonomy and serve Christ as Lord of all your life?

Or do you merely want to live a "comfortable" Christian life—staying in charge yourself, following Christ as long as His plans fit with yours, seeking the best of both worlds? It's certainly possible to seek the Spirit's activity in your life simply to make yourself more comfortable or to enhance your own ego.

Jesus said, "Blessed are those who hunger and thirst for righteousness, for they will be filled" (Matthew 5:6). Do you want the Holy Spirit to so dominate your life to the point that every fiber of your being is brought into submission to the will of God? You have to want to be filled with the Spirit to be filled with the Spirit.

Step Two: Surrender

If you want to be filled, the second step in the process is to get yourself internally positioned to move into the kind of relational space in which the Spirit can take control. This requires making sure you have dethroned ego or self and enthroned Christ as Lord in your life.

This step requires an act of the will. I choose to bow my knee to Christ's lordship. I assess my inner state and make what I call a throne check. I choose to dethrone my own will and ego and invite Christ to reign as Lord. Think of the two throne illustrations we looked at, and let the second represent your heart attitude (see Figure 3.3). This logically brings us to the next step.

Step Three: Ask

The amazing thing about our relationship with Christ is that often all we have to do to receive what God and we ourselves want is to ask. This is certainly true when it comes to being filled with the Spirit. Jesus once said, "If you then, being evil, know how to give good gifts to your children, how much more will your heavenly Father give the Holy Spirit to those who ask him" (Luke 11:13).

In an attitude of prayer, we simply ask the Holy Spirit to fill our lives. We are expressing the fact that we (1) want this caliber of relationship and (2) have positioned ourselves to move into this reality. Again, I cannot emphasize enough that at this point we should not think of the Holy Spirit as a force or substance that we are getting more or less of. He is a person, and we are inviting Him into a state of relationship in which He is free to influence our lives to the greatest degree. Now He can manifest the life of Christ through us, moment by moment.

Step Four: Believe

This is the step of faith. If we have asked with sincerity and integrity of heart, the Holy Spirit fills our lives. By faith, we should thank Him that He has answered our prayer and is in control. I might not feel like a thing has changed at the moment, but what I feel has nothing to do with what God has done.

Faith brings the reality into my experience. As a young Christian, I struggled tremendously with this fact. I kept asking the Holy Spirit to fill my life and kept thinking that something surely must be wrong, because I didn't feel any different. I would go through the day doubting that I was filled with the Spirit and having very little evidence that the Spirit was working in and through my life. I didn't sense that I was empowered, and I didn't see much of the fruit.

One morning all that changed. I now believe that the Holy Spirit was teaching me a very important lesson. At the time, I thought it was an idea of my own invention. I simply decided that after asking to be filled, I would begin to thank God that He had answered my prayer and I was filled. I didn't realize that doing this was the most simple demonstration of faith I could make. The very day I began this practice, my experience began to change.

Within days, I no longer doubted that I was filled. I began to understand in a deeper way that I was filled and that God always answers this prayer because it is His will, and He always answers prayer according to His will (see 1 John 5:13-14). I began to have confidence in the power of the Spirit at work in my life and started seeing more tangible manifestations of His working in and through me. I also saw spiritual fruit being produced through my life.

Putting It All Together

The above process can become second nature to us. In one microsecond we can move through these steps barely thinking about them. In the instant I am conscious of my need to be under the Spirit's control and empowerment, I simply ask. In the same instant, I relinquish control consciously and in faith believe that God answers. It becomes second nature—like breathing. As this becomes an ongoing reality in my life, I begin to live in a state of being continually filled with the Spirit.

All of this is the norm for a man or woman of the Spirit. The filling will be reflected in the evidence of a certain kind of "produce" in his life. This is the subject Paul teaches the believers in the churches of Galatia. He calls this product the fruit of the Spirit. Understanding and experiencing this dimension of the Holy Spirit's work will be our challenge in the next chapter.

ASSIGNMENT: CHAPTER THREE

Personal Application

1. Memorize Ephesians 5:18.
2. Evaluate which of the throne positions most often characterizes your daily living.
3. Begin asking the Holy Spirit to fill your life with His presence and power.

Group Discussion

1. What has been your past experience with trying—daily—to live by God's will? What has helped you the most? What things have tripped you up?
2. In your opinion, what is the difference between "trying to be good" and being filled with the Spirit?
3. What, for you, is the most confusing part of being filled with the Spirit?
4. What things in your life would change if you were "continually being filled with the Spirit?"
5. How do you think a non-Christian would view a Spirit-filled believer? Would seekers likely be turned off by this person's attitudes or his "holiness"? Explain.
6. Would a person necessarily need to know when they are filled with the Spirit? Why, or why not?
7. What person, for you, is the best example of someone who seems to live daily by the Spirit? Describe this person.

CHAPTER 4

WALKING IN THE SPIRIT

"But I say, walk in the Spirit, and you will not fulfill the lusts of the flesh."
—Galatians 5:16

JACK HAD BARELY SURVIVED a terribly frustrating day at work, including a bad meeting with his staff at the end of the day. He'd lost his temper and had come close to storming out because the others hadn't wanted to go along with his plans. Then, on the way home, he'd handled small snags in traffic in a way that didn't quite fit a guy who was trying to follow Christ.

Fortunately, Jack was meeting at 5:00 with his support group at church. As he shared his day with the other men in the group he was surprised that his best buddy, Rich, was offering no sympathy. Instead, Rich simply said, "Sounds to me like you've been walking in the flesh." Rather than responding with the personally directed expletive that immediately came to mind, Jack took a minute to think about Rich's comment.

"You're right," he said.

THE CONFLICT

Being a man or woman of the Spirit is no easy task. It is actually impossible. Impossible, that is, except for Christ in us making it possible.

Like Jack, the constant possibility exists for us to get off track in our relationship with the Lord. We all struggle with an internal conflict that led the apostle Paul to instruct and encourage the brothers in Galatia to "walk in the Spirit" (Galatians 5:16). The alternative is to find ourselves in a condition the Bible identifies as being "in the flesh". To live more consistently in the Spirit, understanding the dynamics involved in these two spiritual states is one of the most important lessons we can learn.

When I talk with men who often experience situations like Jack's, I tell them that I have some good news and some bad news. The good news is this: Christ is in you. The bad news is: *You* are still in you. The existence of these two internal realities creates the conflict Paul addresses in the fifth chapter of Galatians.

Paul begins verse 16 by instructing the Galatians to "walk in the Spirit." The word translated "walk" or "live by" is the Greek word *peripateo*. It literally means "to walk" in the physical sense of ordering your steps. Metaphorically, it was often used to refer to how a person lived his or her life.

The exhortation to walk in the Spirit is offered as the way to avoid carrying out what Paul identifies as "the works of the flesh." We have already seen that through the presence of the Holy Spirit in our lives Christ lives in us. However, along with Christ, we still occupy our lives, and this creates the reality the Bible calls the flesh. *Sarx* is the Greek word translated "flesh" here. The word was used in three different ways in the culture of Paul's day. The primary meaning of *sarx* refers to the physical tissue of the body, as in the expression "flesh and blood." You might remember that after He rose from the dead, Jesus appeared to the disciples and told them to touch Him, so they would know He wasn't a ghost. Jesus said, "Touch me and see; a ghost does not have flesh and bones, as you see I have" (Luke 24:39). The word translated "flesh" in this text is *sarx*.

Sarx was also used symbolically as a metaphor for all humanity. "All flesh is like grass," Peter wrote, quoting the prophet Isaiah (1 Peter 1:24). Again *sarx* appears, but this time in a symbolic manner.

The third use of the word appears primarily in the writings of the Apostle Paul. Paul used this word repeatedly to speak of that part of the person's inner nature, developed apart from a relationship with God, which tends to be the source of inclinations that are still opposed to the will of God. Sometimes the newer translations refer to this reality as the old nature, or sin nature.

In vivid language Paul tells the story: "The flesh desires what is contrary (literally "lusts against") to the Spirit, and the Spirit what is contrary to the flesh" (Galatians 5:17). He goes on to say, "They are in conflict with (literally "hostile to") each other."

This is another good news/bad news reality. The good news is that this conflict is normative. The bad news is that this conflict is normative. Every man or woman seeking to follow Christ will experience it. When you are discouraged about your struggle, you should be encouraged that you are having it! Before coming into relationship with Jesus, you probably didn't even struggle. The fact that you are struggling to be His man or woman is a sign that you *are* His man or woman. Even though this conflict is normative, it's a battle we're expected to win.

Understanding the Struggle

The first step in winning the conflict is to understand the origin and nature of the struggle. It goes all the way back again to the creation story. In chapter 2 of this book I traced the origins of spiritual death. You saw that we were created to be three-dimensional people. You probably remember that the picture we used to illustrate this truth looked like Figure 4.1 below. After the events of Genesis 3, the picture changed to look like Figure 4.2.

As a consequence of the Fall, humanity was born spiritually dead. The Holy Spirit was no longer present in the human spirit. The result of this condition radically affected the moral, spiritual, physical, and emotional development of all men and women from that point in human history forward. In the first chapter of Genesis, God said, "Let us make man in our image" (Genesis 1:26).

Figure 4.1: Three-dimensional Man

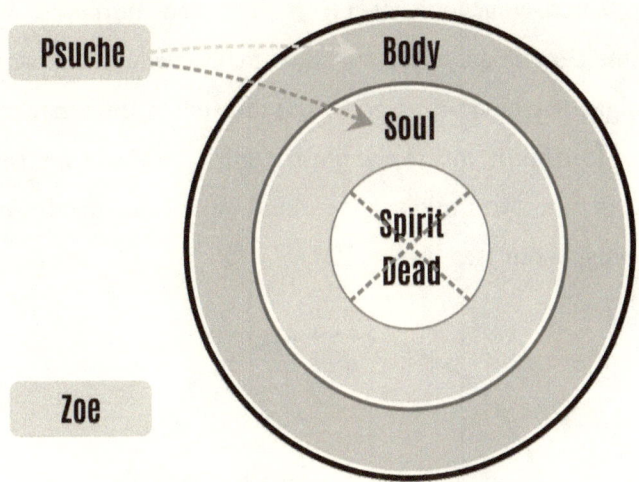

Figure 4.2: Spiritual Death

Then we are told, "God created man in his own image, in the image of God he created him" (verse 27). You might remember that in chapter 2 I made reference to a text in Genesis 5 where we are given an account of Adam's descendants following the Fall. A very subtle nuance in the language here is of immense significance.

In verse 1 of chapter 5, the writer of Genesis reminds us that "when God created man, he made him in the likeness of God." Then, in verse 3, we are told, "When Adam had lived 130 years, he had a son *in his own likeness*" (italics added). The image of God had been distorted to become the image of fallen man. What does this mean?

When you look at God's intended purposes, it seems clear that the process of human development was designed to be dominated by the indwelling influence of the Holy Spirit within the human spirit. Again, if we use our graphic, you might chart the flow of influence from the inside out (see Figure 4.3).

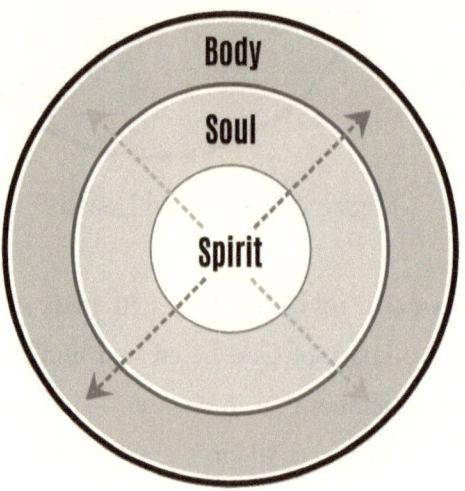

Figure 4.3: Flow of Influence

Under this scenario, the soul of the human—his or her emotions, intellect, and will—would have been shaped by the influence of God's Spirit. The image of God would have been imprinted on each person at birth and throughout the developmental stages. The soul would have been in submission to the Spirit, and the body would function as the servant of both.

What happened after the Fall? My own sense is that the flow of influence was inverted. Without the Spirit present, the dominant influence became the body. Its desires, needs, and passions became an inordinate influence on the development of the soul. No longer was the human a reflection of God; he now reflected his fallen forefather, Adam.

Fallen humanity developed apart from the influence of the Spirit of God with the result that our inner life, or soul, including our intellectual, emotional, and habitual development, became distorted. The product of this faulty development is an inner nature that is out of conformity with the will of God and desires ways of living that are in conflict with the ways of the Spirit. In other words, this is the *sarx*—the flesh, or old nature, or sin nature.

When we become Christians, in the biblical sense of that word, our lives are invaded by the Holy Spirit. He is the source of a new internal reality theologians call the new nature. The new nature is a product of the Spirit working in our intellect, emotions, and will to transform us into the men and women God wants us to be.

At the point of regeneration or spiritual birth, we begin a lifelong process of spiritual reclamation and transformation that is intended to once again help us become conformed to the image of Christ. All spiritual growth is targeted toward this end. This is God's ultimate will for your life. The Bible states, "For those God foreknew he also predestined to be conformed to the image of his Son" (Romans 8:29).

When you see how radically different these two parts of our inner landscape are, it becomes clear why there is conflict. It also becomes clear why we experience so much difficulty in our spiritual growth. The first step in winning the conflict is to identify when we are operating out of the old nature, and then to understand how to shift into the new.

Identifying the Flesh

In this passage in Galatians 5, Paul gives us a great tool for learning how to tell when we are living in the flesh and when we are walking in the Spirit. Each of these two internal realties produces distinct behaviors. Paul calls the outcomes of living under the dominant influence of the old nature the works or deeds of the flesh. He calls the outcomes of living under the dominant influence of the Spirit the fruit of the Spirit.

In verses 19 through 21 Paul lists a series of behaviors that can serve as a checklist for knowing when our behavior is a product of the dominant influence of the flesh. These characteristics will always be the outcome of our old ego taking control of our life. Remember that to be filled with the Spirit we must allow Christ to reign on the inner throne. This spiritual state was represented in chapter 3 by the illustration below (see Figure 4.4).

When through neglect of our spiritual state or some blatant act of disobedience we dethrone Christ and enthrone ego, our inner life can be characterized by Figure 4.5.

✝ - Christ is in the life and on the throne
S - Self is yielding to Christ

Figure 4.4: Christ Enthroned

S - Self is on the throne
✝ - Christ is outside the life

Figure 4.5 Christ Dethroned

It is when ego or self gets back into control that the flesh produces its works. Ego-controlled and "in the flesh" are synonymous terms. Here are the outcomes of this condition: immorality, impurity, debauchery, idolatry, witchcraft, hatred, discord, jealousy, rage, selfish ambition, dissensions, factions, envy, drunkenness, orgies.

Just in case Paul missed a few, he throws in the expression "and the like" as a summary phrase. It is another way of saying, "You get the picture." These fifteen-plus behaviors can be reduced to five general categories to help us identify when we are operating out of the flesh.

Category #1—Immorality

The flesh is immoral. It will take God-given drives such as sexuality and create a desire so strong that we will be tempted to fulfill those desires outside the boundaries and conditions God has established. Thus normal and healthy desires become warped and produce painful consequences in our lives.

Category #2—Idolatry

The flesh is idolatrous. It serves false gods. When we operate out of the flesh we will tend to value something other than Christ as the most important priority in our life. It is interesting that in this passage in Galatians, Paul identifies greed as idolatry. In other words, you don't need a literal golden cow to practice idolatry. The passion for possessions, power, prestige, or pleasure can all become idols in our lives.

Category #3—Destruction

The flesh is destructive. It tends to be murderous and violent. Sometimes this inclination takes overtly physical forms. Hatred, rage, and violent behavior such as physical abusiveness are products of the flesh. At other times, the destructive nature of the flesh is less obvious. Slander, malice, and gossip are destructive verbal actions that harm others. Both literal assassination and character assassination are generated by the flesh.

Category #4—Lewdness

The flesh is crude. In language and action it exhibits behavior that is morally repugnant. It is the antonym of wholesomeness.

Category #5—Self-Centered

Above all else, the flesh is selfish and egocentric. It is "me" focused and blind to the needs of others. It operates out of a narcissistic self-love that is ultimately destructive to others and to the person who is living in the flesh. It carries within itself the seeds of its own destruction.

Whenever our emotions or behavior are dominated by these five characteristics, we can be quite sure we are operating out of the flesh. The ability to understand this reality will take us a long way toward solving the problem of walking in the flesh instead of walking in the Spirit.

THE SOLUTION

Understanding the flesh leads us naturally to learning how to identify when we are operating out of it. This brings us to a very important concept that is critical in learning how to walk in the Spirit.

We have seen that these two internal realities—the flesh and the Spirit, the old nature and the new nature— are present within the life of every true believer. They constitute what we might call spiritual states. The processing unit God has built into each of our lives to help us understand, identify, and then decide which state we will respond to, is the mind.

God has created us with the capacity to be self-conscious. It is one of the qualities that separates us from the rest of the animal kingdom. Dogs or cats are created beings as we are, but they are not self-conscious. They do not have the capability to step back from their lives and assess and evaluate their behavior. You and I do. This can be both a blessing and a curse. In this case, it's a blessing. Picture the complexity of your internal "landscape" as illustrated in Figure 4.6.

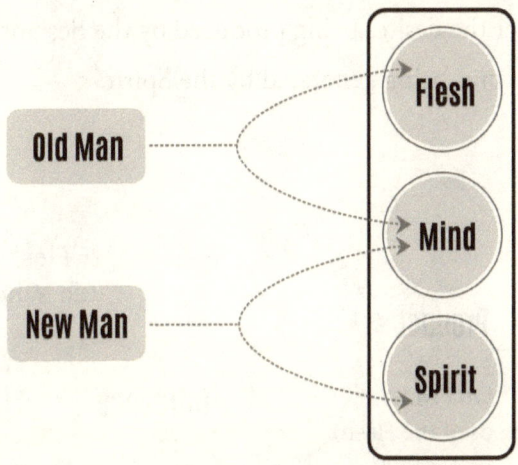

Figure 4.6: Internal Drive Structure

Notice that in the diagram the mind is positioned between the flesh and the Spirit. In the book of Romans, Paul speaks of the mind set on the flesh and the mind set on the Spirit: "For those who live according to the [flesh] set their *minds* on the what the flesh desires; but those who live in the Spirit have their *minds set* on what the Spirit desires" (Romans 8:5, italics added).

Put this verse together with the passage in Galatians. First, we have a clear statement regarding the struggle. Two natures, the flesh and the Spirit, are in conflict. Then we are given an inventory to help us understand and identify the two different propensities. Now we are told that the mind is the controlling factor that responds to either the desires being produced by the flesh or to the promptings being generated by the Spirit.

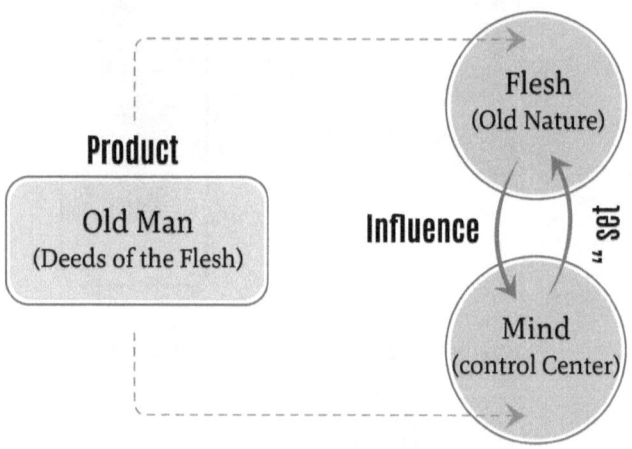

Figure 4.7: In the Flesh

When the mind is set on—or chooses to respond to—the flesh, we live out of the old nature and bear its fruit. Although not a perfect representation, we could diagram the pattern as in Figure 4.7.

The alternative is to operate from a mind set on the
Spirit. In the book of Colossians, Paul instructs us, "Set
your minds on things above" (Colossians 3:2). In another
passage he encourages us to "have this mind in you which
was also in Christ Jesus" (Philippians 2:5). In all these
instances we see that we have a choice to make. We
decide. We set our minds. God has given us the ability
to have a choice in this matter and the ability to say no
to the flesh and yes to the Spirit. This "mind-set" can be
illustrated as in Figure 4.8 below.

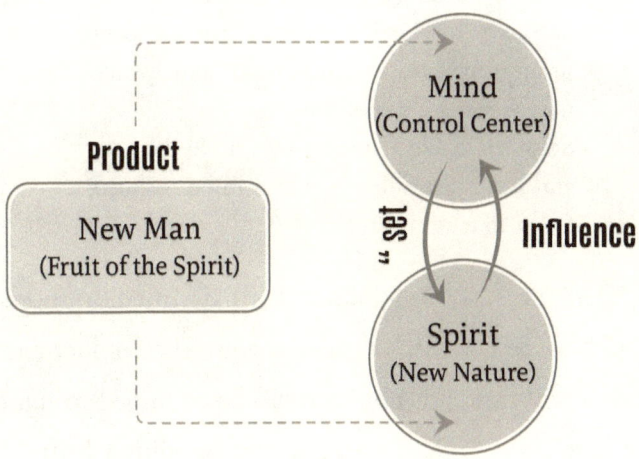

Figure 4.8: In the Spirit

Having the mind set on the Spirit means that we
use the freedom that is ours to say no to the old nature

and yes to the Spirit. We choose to respond to the Spirit
and do that which we know to be consistent with His
promptings and instruction. Every time we make this
choice, we take a step. As step-by-step we choose to
follow Christ, we begin walking in the Spirit. Here is a
simple reminder of the three steps we take to walk in the
Spirit:

> **Step 1:** *Understand.* Understand the feelings,
> desires, and behaviors that originate out of
> the Spirit and those that are a product of the
> flesh.
>
> **Step 2:** *Identify.* At any given moment,
> be able to identify which nature your
> promptings are coming from and which
> nature you are responding to.
>
> **Step 3:** *Decide.* Choose to say no to the flesh
> and yes to the Spirit. Set your mind. Ask the
> Spirit to take control.

Over time, as you follow this pattern, the process
should become second nature to you. The conflict and
tension will not end, but you will be equipped to fight
the fight. As you mature and practice keeping Christ on
the throne, you can expect to become more sensitive to
these dynamics. Sensitivity develops with maturity and
practice. As you become more consistent in walking in
the Spirit, you will begin to notice a difference in what

is being produced by your life. You will begin to see how God is working through you to bear the fruit of the Spirit. Understanding this dimension of the spiritual life will be our task in the next chapter.

ASSIGNMENT: CHAPTER FOUR

Personal Application

1. Read Galatians 5 every day this week.
2. Make a list of the deeds of the flesh and the fruit of the Spirit. Carry the list with you and look it over several times during the day.
3. Begin to consciously evaluate which of the two spiritual states your behavior is being generated by.

Group Discussion

1. What is your overall reaction to this chapter? Are there any concepts with which you strongly agree or disagree? Why?
2. Share about a time when you were apparently acting in response to the promptings of the Spirit. Share about a time when your behavior was "in the flesh." Describe the difference.
3. In God's eyes, is the body bad? In what sense is "the flesh" immoral?
4. Suppose a person says to you, "Being filled with the Spirit sounds like you have to go around all day keeping a scorecard for every little thought and action. Where's the spontaneity, the zest for living? I say, just live your life and be happy!" How would you respond?

5. In the struggle with the flesh, how do you, personally, win the battle? What helps you the most? When you fail, what is the main reason?

6. Where do you place the person who has an addiction (say, to alcohol or pornography) in this scheme of things?

7. In your opinion, how can a person overcome an addiction? If you have seen it happen, tell about it!

CHAPTER 5

THE FRUIT OF THE SPIRIT

"But the fruit of the Spirit is . . ."
—Galatians 5:22

I USED TO LIVE IN SANTACRUZ,CALIFORNIA. Someone once told me that when God created heaven, He used Santa Cruz as a model. They were wrong, of course. But the area surrounding Monterey Bay is one of the most scenic pieces of geography in the world. I used to love riding my motorcycle on Highway 1 as it heads both north and south out of town. To the north, the road leads straight to San Francisco and up the coast toward Seattle. To the south, you ride past Monterey, Carmel, and Big Sur as you head toward L.A. and San Diego.

Today the Santa Cruz area and its neighbor San Jose are known as the high-tech center of the West Coast.

Many of my former neighbors and friends make the daily drive "over the hill" to work at places like Apple, Hewlett-Packard, and Google. But the area is also famous for "software" of another type.

If you aren't from the Bay area, you've probably never heard of Castroville, but it's the "Artichoke Capital of the World." Driving through town on Highway 1, you see fields on both sides of the road filled with ripe artichoke plants. Farther north, roadside stands proliferate, selling fresh strawberries, peaches, apples, and nearly every variety of fruit and vegetable imaginable. Pass over the Golden Gate bridge and you can head inland to the Napa and Sonoma valleys and view sun-drenched panoramas bursting with the fruit of the vine.

This is agricultural Mecca.

Fruitful.

That is the word that comes to mind as you cruise past field after field, framed by ocean on one side and mountain and hill on the other. This land was created to bear fruit. How tragic it would be to pass these same fields and find them dry and barren, no longer fulfilling their designed purpose. You'd miss the sweet flavor of the strawberry or the enjoyment of sinking your teeth into a freshly steamed leaf of artichoke just dipped in warm butter.

THE FRUIT OF THE SPIRIT

The ground of the spiritual life is much like the land around the San Francisco and Monterey bays. It is intended to be fruitful. Since Jesus lived in an agricultural society, He often used images from the fields to teach spiritual truths. The night before His death, as He shared the Passover meal with His disciples, He told them, "I AM the vine; you are the branches. If a man abides in me and I in him, he will bear much fruit" (John 15:5). He went on to say that the very reason He had chosen them was that they might "go and produce fruit" (verse 16).

The spiritual life is intended to produce certain qualities that the Bible calls fruit. Our lives are intended to be fruitful, that is, productive. In the fifth chapter of Galatians, the apostle Paul describes for us what our "fruit" is to be.

This is one of the most helpful passages in all of the New Testament. It is like an inventory God has provided to help us figure out whether or not we're on the right track. In the Galatians 5 passage, we find a contrast between the product of that old nature, called the "flesh," and the fruit of the new part of our being created by the presence of the Holy Spirit.

In the last chapter we looked at what happens when the fallen part of our nature controls our lives. Let's review that list again, taken from Galatians 5:19-21, and make it into a real "checklist."

_____	Immorality	_____	rage
_____	Impurity	_____	Selfish Ambition
_____	Debauchery	_____	Dissensions
_____	Idolatry	_____	Factions
_____	Witchcraft	_____	Envy
_____	Hatred	_____	Drunkenness
_____	Discord	_____	Orgies
_____	Jealousy		

These are the products of a life lived under the control of the ego, or self. Can you check off any of these as traits that permeate your being? If these are the qualities that characterize your life, you can pretty much figure that it's not the Holy Spirit controlling your life.

Having identified these problematic behaviors, Paul goes on to give us another checklist of what *should* characterize our lives if the Holy Spirit really is in control. He calls these traits the fruit of the Spirit:

_____	Love	_____	Goodness
_____	Joy	_____	Gentleness
_____	Peace	_____	Faithfulness

_____ Patience   _____ Self-Control
_____ Kindness

What a contrast! It is one of those places in the Bible where you have a sense that God is asking, "What do you want? Do you want your life to look like this—hatred, jealousy, immorality, hatred, and the like? Or do you want your life to be characterized by love, joy, and peace?"

If you are reading this book, you're probably trying to figure out how to spend more time on list number two and less on list number one. If the Holy Spirit is the dominant influence in your life, you should expect to see an increase in the fruit of the Spirit and a decrease in the deeds or works of the flesh. Let's take a closer look at each of the characteristics of the fruit of the Spirit.

Love

The dominant fruit, or product, of the Holy Spirit is love. In a very real sense, all of the other dimensions of the fruit flow from this quality. For instance, if we are committed to loving someone, let's say our wives, we will be kind and gentle with them. Love is the mark of a man or woman of the Spirit. You might not think you are a very loving person. That might be the case, but you might also misunderstand the kind of love this passage proclaims.

The word translated "love" in this verse is the Greek word *agape*. This is not the warm, fuzzy feeling you had the first time your sweetheart, later to become your husband or wife, kissed you good night. That would be an emotion best represented in the Greek language by the word *phileo*. Nor is it the passion you felt for your husband or wife the first time you consummated your wedding vows. That kind of love is expressed by use of the biblical word *eros*.

Agape is a different kind of love. It is not merely emotional or physical in origin. The word means "to seek the highest welfare of another." It is an unconditional type of love that is also self-sacrificial. If the welfare of another is costly to me, *agape* is willing to pay the price. It is a supernatural love made possible in my life by . . . guess who? The Holy Spirit. In his letter to his friends in Rome, Paul taught that "The love of God [*agape*] has been poured out into our hearts by the Holy Spirit, whom he has given us" (Romans 5:5).

The great love chapter of the New Testament, 1 Corinthians 13, identifies sixteen characteristics of this kind of love:

Agape is:

Patient
Kind

Not envious
Not boastful
Not proud
Not rude
Not self-seeking
Not easily angered
Keeps no record of wrongs
Does not delight in evil
Rejoices with the truth
Always protects
Always trusts
Always hopes
Always perseveres
Never fails

This is a tremendous list of qualities! Only God could create this kind of love. Only God does. Love is the dominant characteristic of the fruit of the Spirit. The other eight dimensions of the fruit flow from love.

Joy

Joy is an internal experience of grace. The word translated joy in the book of Galatians is the word *chara*. It comes from the same root as the word *charis*, which we translate as "grace." We most often identify it with happiness. When we think of a joyful person, we often think of someone with a smile on his or her face, someone who seems to be happy. Joy is more than this.

Happiness is an emotional experience. It is usually produced by some external circumstance that has generated the feeling. Joy goes deeper. Joy is a spiritual reality. It is a product of being in the proper relationship with God. Joy transcends circumstance. It is possible to have joy even when circumstances are quite difficult.

Peace

Peace is a state of inner well-being. It is the product of the Holy Spirit's influence in our inner life when our relationship with God is in a proper state. The word means much more than the absence of strife.

The Hebrew word for peace is *shalom*. The Greek word *eirene* is the New Testament equivalent. *Shalom* is a total state of well-being that includes the physical, emotional, spiritual, and relational dimensions of life. In the Old Testament, this reality was intimately related to God's blessing. When God blessed a person, the resulting experience was peace. When you are experiencing God's peace, it will be manifested by the sense of serenity, tranquility, and contentment that only the Spirit of God can produce in your life.

Patience

There are several words in the Greek New Testament translated by the English word "patience." This particular word is *makrothumia*, sometimes translated "long-suffering." It is a relational word that speaks of the ability to endure the flaws of another and stay committed to the relationship.

Long-suffering is one of the characteristics of *agape* love highlighted in the famous love passage of 1 Corinthians 13. To be patient with others requires that we see beyond their surface behavior to the heart of who they are as people loved by God. If treated rudely, the patient man doesn't immediately respond with irritability. He asks the question, "What is going on with this person that is causing him or her to behave like this?" Patience opens the door to enable us to respond with the next dimension of the fruit.

Kindness

Kindness is one of the most beautiful expressions of the work of the Spirit in our lives. The word *chrestotes* is sometimes translated as "goodness" or "gentleness." These three words—kindness, goodness, and gentleness—are closely related. Together they produce a man or woman who aggressively seeks to care for others. Kindness fanatically avoids inflicting pain on others, and then seeks to express tenderness and compassion by doing something good for the person. A kind man or woman is a tremendous witness to the character of Christ.

Goodness

Goodness is closely related to kindness. The word *agathosune* speaks of actively expressing the love of God in acts of generosity. Goodness is much like grace in its expression. Grace is an undeserved gift. Goodness is a quality that seeks to meet a person's need regardless of whether he or she deserves it.

It's easier to understand goodness when you know its opposite. The antonym of goodness is the Greek word *poneros*, which is sometimes translated by our words "evil" or "wicked." At its root, *poneros* means stingy or miserly. It is the quality of the person who has no concern for the welfare of another.

In the early years of the Christian church, the Roman Emperor Hadrian wanted to understand what Christians were all about. He asked a man named Aristides, who wrote the following:

> *They love one another. They never fail to help widows; they save orphans from those who would hurt them. If they have something, they give freely to the man who has nothing. If they*

> see a stranger, they take him home, and are
> happy as though he were a real brother. They
> don't consider themselves brothers in the usual
> sense, but brothers instead through the Spirit,
> in God.

That's goodness!

Faithfulness

Faithfulness is rooted in the Greek word *pistis*, which we translate "faith." In this context the word has two dimensions, or directions, that define its meaning. One direction of the word is horizontal—a quality describing our relationship with other men. To be faithful in this context means to be loyal or trustworthy. A man or woman who bears this dimension of the Spirit's fruit is a person whose help we can rely on, whose loyalty we can count on, and upon whose word we can depend.

The other direction of this word is vertical, referring to a man's relationship with God. A faithful man or woman maintains an ongoing posture of faith. He believes God and continually surrenders and commits himself to God's will. This is the kind of man Paul admonishes Timothy to invest his life in (2 Timothy 2:2).

Gentleness

Gentleness is one of our English translations of the Greek word *prautes*. Sometimes it is also translated "meekness." Neither English word does a very good job of capturing the thrust of *prautes*, which has been defined as "strength under control." The Greek word was used of a wild horse who had been trained and domesticated so that all of its strength could now be put at the disposal of its master. When we understand this as the meaning of the word, we get a little more of a feel for why Moses was called the meekest man who ever lived (Numbers 12:3).

Jesus referred to himself as meek, and yet we see how He stood up in the face of the religious hypocrites of his day and called them whitewashed tombs full of dead men's bones (Matthew 23:27). *Prautes* is the characteristic of the Spirit's influence that motivates and enables us to bring all of our gifts, abilities, talents, strengths, and resources to God and then give Him control over them. It is the quality that leads to a submitted life.

Self-Control

The final dimension of the fruit is self-control. If *prautes* refers to strength under control, then we could think of this quality as ego under control. The Greeks used this word, *enkrateia*, to describe one who has a grip on one's self. It was the ability to control impulse and passion. When a man or woman possesses this quality they can refrain from wrong and engage in what is right. It is a spiritual quality that is the same as the discipline a great athlete has over his body.

When you put these nine qualities or characteristics together, you have a picture of the kind of man or woman the Holy Spirit is attempting to make you. And when we look at the big picture, we can see why Paul is able to say that against such things there is no law. The Law was put into effect to be a restraint against the kind of behavior that destroys life and relationships.

When we are actively bearing the fruit, we really don't need the Law. There is no need for an external standard when the internal reality of our lives looks like this. The big question becomes: How do I produce these qualities? What is my part, and what is God's part?

BEARING FRUIT

It isn't enough to know what the fruit of the Spirit is. We need to know how to produce it. The process involves what I call spiritual will-power. Let me explain. The kind of will-power I am referring to is different from what we usually mean when we use this expression. Often, will-power speaks only of what we can accomplish by the sheer force of our own resources. Spiritual will-power is a totally different process. It involves a person's will *and* God's power. It is the perfect mix for producing spiritual fruit.

One passage of the Bible that illustrates this process is Philippians 2:12-13. Here Paul instructs the believers in Philippi to "work out your salvation with fear and trembling, for it is God who is at work in you to desire and to act according to his good purpose."

This text shows us the balance of God's part and our part in the process of living the spiritual life. God is at work in us so that we can work it out. The Holy Spirit is present in our inner lives. He is enabling us to produce the nine characteristics of the fruit of the Spirit. In a sense, He *is* the nine characteristics. His presence in us makes us capable of expressing these qualities.

We also have a part to play. Our job is to "work out" that which God is working within. This is where the tricky balance of dependence and obedience becomes critical. I can't love with *agape* love apart from Christ in me, enabling me to love that way. But the reality of love will not be manifested until, in obedience, I choose to express it in tangible ways. John tells us not to love in words only, but in deed and in truth (1 John 3:18).

Notice that nearly every dimension of the fruit of the Spirit is a quality about which some other part of the

New Testament instructs or commands us to take action. For instance, Jesus commanded us to "love one another" (John 13:35). His part is to make this possible in our inner being; our part is to step out in dependence upon His enabling power and act in love.

Let's say I come home from a very difficult day at work. I want to get in a fetal position and read the paper or watch the news. My son comes to me and asks, "Dad, can we play catch?" What is the loving action? I don't feel very loving. I don't really want to play catch. But if I sense my son really needs my time and attention, I can make a choice. I can ask Christ to empower me to love my son by playing catch. I can choose to act according to love, not according to selfish desire.

Let's go a step further. Suppose my wife tells me that I'm not treating her properly. She claims I'm short with her when she attempts to talk to me about some problem she senses in our relationship. Perhaps she claims I never listen to her and that our marriage lacks good communication. (usually this kind of interaction takes place in a much more heated emotional setting.) How do we handle these encounters?

I have to confess that at such times I don't feel very loving. My initial tendency is to become defensive and explain to my wife why her observations are not completely accurate. Of course, this exchange tends to be emotionally charged, and my choice of words might not accurately communicate my concern in an appropriate manner.

The stage is now set to choose love. I can pray and ask Christ to help me love my wife as I need to. I can choose to say no to my negative feelings and choose to take time to listen without defensiveness in a sincere attempt to understand her needs.

Let's go one step further. Suppose an elderly man in the neighborhood has let his house run down to the point that it's become an eyesore to the neighborhood. This particular man has been less than a model neighbor. As a matter of fact, he has alienated everyone in the neighborhood at one time or another. How do you love him? You *choose* to love him. Perhaps you organize a group from your church to come and clean his yard and paint his house. That would be love.

Love requires decision and action. The Holy Spirit can enable us to love with *agape* love, but you and I have to exercise our wills and take the loving action.

What is true of love is true of the other fruit. To bear joy, we are required to rejoice. "Rejoice in the Lord always. Again I will say, rejoice!" (Philippians 4:4). To rejoice means to be joyful. Remember, joy is more than mere happiness (an emotional state that often we cannot control). Joy is a spiritual reality that requires an act of the will on our part.

Peace is a product of the Holy Spirit at work in our lives. It is also a state that we are called to cultivate: "And let the peace of Christ rule in your hearts" (Colossians 3:15).

The same is true of patience: "Be patient" (James 5:7).

Kindness: "Be kind to everyone" (2 Timothy 2:24).

Gentleness: "Let your gentleness be known to all men" (Philippians 4:5).

Faithfulness: "Be faithful unto death" (Revelation 2:10)

Goodness: "Do good unto all" (Galatians 6:10).

Over and over we are instructed to initiate these behaviors. We are to depend on God to be at work within us to transform our hearts and give us the ability to take these actions, but we have to step out in faith and attempt to "do the stuff," as someone has expressed it.

The bottom line on bearing fruit is to learn to stay in the kind of relationship with Christ in which the Spirit is most able to do His part, and then to express that relationship through obedient action. This quality of relationship is called "abiding" in the Bible. It is the translation of the Greek word *meno*, meaning "to settle down and make yourself at home." Jesus promised that if we would abide in Him and He in us, we would bear much fruit (John 15:5).

Immediately after making this promise, He went on to say, "If you keep my commandments, you will abide in my love" (John 15:10). Then He gave a specific command regarding one dimension of the fruit, "These things I command you: that you love one another" (John 15:17).

Every action produced by this kind of process will make us a bit more conformed to the image of Christ, and more a man or woman of the Spirit.

ASSIGNMENT: CHAPTER FIVE

Personal Application

1. Read Galatians 5 every day this week. Attempt to memorize verses 22-23.
2. List the fruit of the Spirit and assess which qualities often characterize your attitudes and actions.
3. This week, look for specific ways to demonstrate love to your immediate family.

Group Discussion

1. What is your experience with will-power, in general? When have you seen "spiritual willpower" at work? Do you agree that it can bring lasting change in a person's life? Why, or why not?
2. In your opinion, what are the pros and cons of making "checklists" of spiritual characteristics? In what practical ways could such lists help you?
3. When have you felt most fruitful in your life? Why?
4. Tell about a time when you seemed to face a "yes or no" choice about whether to follow the Spirit's leading. What happened? What did you learn?
5. What is the difference between committing an act of sin (such as those listed in Galatians 5:19-21) and being *characterized* by such behaviors? Does "not inheriting the kingdom of God" mean that people who commit such sins will not go to heaven? Explain.

6. When have you seen one or more of the fruit of the Spirit shine forth in someone's life?

7. When is it most difficult for you to manifest the fruit of the Spirit? What obstacles (especially at home) seem to be the hardest to overcome? What insight or advice can others in your group offer you?

THE GIFTS OF THE SPIRIT

"Now about spiritual gifts, brothers,
I do not want you to be ignorant."
—I Corinthians 12:1

A NUMBER OF YEARS AGO, my son, Baker, came to me in the first week of January and said, "Dad, do you know what I want next Christmas?" Like many young boys and girls, Baker loved receiving gifts. As a matter of fact, adults love gifts, too. I would be lying if I said that I didn't still love birthdays and Christmas for the very same reasons my children do. I, too, can be tempted to start thinking about Christmas as soon as the New Year's celebrations start winding down.

My favorite gifts have one of two characteristics that endear them to me. The first characteristic involves

98

the giver. My most cherished presents have come from my wife and children. For example, I have two unique-looking pieces of art in my office. One looks a bit like a totem pole, and the other is definitely a bird. Both are made of papier-mâché. To the untrained eye, they might seem of little value. To me, they are priceless. The totem pole (I think that's what it is) was given to me by Stephanie when she was in fifth grade. The bird (I'm sure that's what it is!) was a Father's Day gift from my son Baker. The value of the gifts, in this case, is directly related to the identity of the givers.

The second characteristic that determines how much I like a gift is its intrinsic value. I remember one Christmas, as a teenager, when my mom decided I was old enough to receive only "practical" gifts. I think I opened a half-dozen packages of underwear and socks that year. I was the youngest example of Ebenezer Scrooge you have ever seen.

In contrast, the most intrinsically valuable gift I have ever been given came from a group of men in the Bible study I taught for fifteen years. One afternoon I was invited by one of the men to come to his office "to give him some advice." He was the president of a large company in Denver, and I felt honored. When I arrived at the office, he took me into a conference room where twenty men had gathered to present me with a brand-new Harley Davidson motorcycle. I can't describe how I felt. It was the first time in my life that I was truly speechless. I valued this gift for the love and appreciation it expressed on behalf of the men, but let's face it, it was one heck of a lot more meaningful than if they had given me a box of underwear with "Good job!" written on a card.

You might think my approach to gift appreciation is too materialistic, but I think most of us would agree that the criteria I've described are relatively common. What's the point? You and I have been given some gifts to which we should attach immense value. The *giver* of these gifts and the *intrinsic worth* of the gifts should make them something we value with all our hearts.

OUR SPIRITUAL GIFTS

As men and women who have come into relationship with Jesus Christ and in whom the Holy Spirit dwells, we have been given gifts by God. They are called *charismata* in the New Testament. This word, which we translate "spiritual gifts," comes from the Greek word *charis*, usually translated "grace." It means "a free gift." *Charismata* are special endowments of God's grace that are a function of the work of the Holy Spirit in our lives.

In other words, you are gifted. It's nice to know, isn't it? You have been endowed with one or more gifts that are to be used to fulfill God's plans and purposes for your life, as they relate to God's plans and purposes for the world.

The Key "Gift Passages"

Four primary passages in the New Testament list spiritual gifts. Whether these lists are all-inclusive or not is a matter of interpretation and opinion. Some scholars believe they are exhaustive, and others believe there could be other gifts, or combinations of gifting, not specifically designated in these passages. Each of the four passages is set in a unique context that can help us categorize the various lists and give us an overview of the *charismata*.

Romans 12:3-8.

This is one of two primary passages that explains and identifies spiritual gifts. It has been suggested that given the foundational nature of the book of Romans, these seven gifts might be the basic building blocks of giftedness within the body of Christ. Those who suggest this also hypothesize that every Christian has one of these seven gifts as his or her primary gift. There is no specific biblical data to support this view, but it is an interesting way to explore the subject.

The seven gifts are:

1. *Prophecy*—the ability to speak forth the Word of God (verse 6)
2. *Serving*—helping with the practical needs of fellow believers (verse 7)
3. *Teaching*—the ability to explain the meaning and application of the Bible (verse 7)
4. *Exhortation*—the special ability to encourage other Christians to take practical action in their Christian growth and service (verse 8)
5. *Giving*—the ability to provide the physical and financial resources necessary to do the work of ministry (verse 8)
6. *Leadership*—the ability to provide organizational and directional leadership to the church and its ministry (verse 8)
7. *Mercy*—a unique compassion to respond to the needs of the broken and wounded (verse 8)

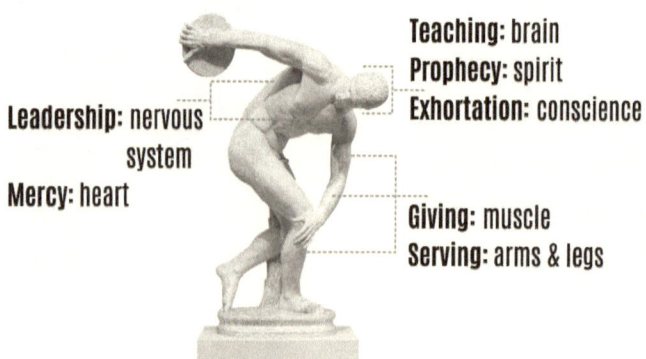

Figure 6.1: The Body at Work

If these are the seven foundational gifts, we might imagine them as parts of the body that would look something like figure 6.1 above.

1 Corinthians 12:1-11.

In addition to the list of gifts in Romans, Paul offered another list when he wrote to the church in Corinth. This congregation was experiencing a minor split over the use of the *charismata*. Apparently, certain members placed inordinate emphasis on the gift of tongues. Paul addresses the problem by giving what is perhaps the most extensive piece of New Testament teaching on the subject of spiritual gifts.

In verse 7, Paul refers to the *charismata* as "manifestations" of the Spirit. Those who view the Romans passage as foundational often refer to those seven gifts as the motivational gifts and these in 1 Corinthians as manifestation gifts. But this theory doesn't maintain complete consistency, because there is a degree of overlap in the lists. The Corinthian list contains nine specific gifts in verses 8-10:

1. *The word of wisdom*—a supernatural insight into how a situation is to be handled (verse 8)
2. *The word of knowledge*—a supernatural revelation of information (verse 8)

3. *Faith*—a special ability to believe that God is going to do something supernatural (verse 9)
4. *Healing*—the ability to be a channel of God's healing power (verse 9)
5. *Miracles*—the ability to perform supernatural acts that override the natural course of events (verse 10)
6. *Prophecy*—the ability to preach or speak forth the Word of God, both in prediction and instruction (verse 10)
7. *Discernment*—the ability to know whether a message or action is of God or from a humanistic or demonic source (verse 10)
8. *Tongues*—the ability to speak in an unlearned foreign language (verse 10)
9. *Interpretation*—the ability to translate a message given in tongues without having learned the language in which the message was given (verse 10)

Later in this passage, Paul makes reference to those who exercise the gifts in certain offices in the church. He seems to be attempting to give a sense of the priority of certain gifts, in order to encourage a more balanced use of the gifts within the church. In these verses Paul mentions two more gifts:

1. *Helps*—a special motivation and ability to help with practical needs, much like the gift of service (verse 28).
2. *Administration*—the ability to organize and orchestrate the ministry of the church (verse 28).

There are some who believe these two gifts might be the same as the gifts of service and leadership mentioned in Romans, but for now, let's keep them separate.

Ephesians 4:7-13.

The third passage dealing with the gifts of the Spirit is found in Ephesians 4. The context of this passage has to do with certain individuals whose task within the church is to equip the other members of the body to fulfill their God-given roles. These are sometimes referred to as the equipping gifts, although it would be more accurate to understand that the "gift" here as the *person* who exercises certain gifts to fulfill the functions of the office. All four of the Ephesian gifts are found in verse 11:

1. *Apostle*—one who is sent forth with the authority of God to proclaim Christ and plant new churches.
2. *Prophet*—one who is called to speak the Word of God with the authority of God.
3. *Evangelist*—the special ability to present the message of salvation with exceptional effectiveness.
4. *Pastor/Teacher*—the ability to care for the members of the body and help them grow through spiritual instruction.

The definition of the function of these gifts follows in the text. Paul writes, "For the equipping of the "saints" for the work of ministry, for the building up of the body of Christ" (verse 12).

1 Peter 4:10-11

This short list is prefaced by a simple definition as to the purpose of the gifts. Peter encourages his audience: "As each one has received a gift, use the gift to minister to one another, as good stewards of the manifold grace of God" (4:10). He then speaks specifically of two gifts:

1. *Speaking*—the ability to communicate spiritual truth.
2. *Serving*—the ability to help with the practical needs of fellow believers.

Putting Them Together

If we put these four passages together, we find somewhere between nineteen and twenty-four specific gifts, depending on how many of the lists contain overlaps. Nowhere are we told that these lists are exhaustive, and the very fact that different gifts are highlighted in different letters to different groups of believers, offers good reason to believe that other gifts exist. But if we look at the scope of the ones mentioned, almost every special capability

God gives could probably be categorized under one of the revealed gifts. Here's the point: Every man or woman, in whom the Spirit has come to dwell, has one or more of these gifts. I am convinced that each of us has a unique mix, or cluster, of gifts given by God to equip us to fulfill our God-designed calling on this planet.

For many of us, one of these gifts will be more dominant than the others. Our most dominant gift will tend to steer us toward the general area of service to which we are called. The other gifts, clustered around our dominant gifting, will enhance and facilitate the specific ministry God has prepared for us to accomplish.

DISCOVERING YOUR GIFTS

Once you begin to understand what the Bible teaches about spiritual gifts, the logical response is to want to know what your own gifts are. How do you discover your gifting?

Many excellent books deal with the subject of spiritual gifts, and most of them offer some kind of process for gift discovery. Many books even contain tests, like the Modified Houts Inventory, developed by Fuller Seminary, to help steer you in the right direction.

Over the years, I have reached a few conclusions of my own concerning the process of discovering gifts. I find that resources like books and tests are helpful, but I am convinced that the two keys to discovering our gifts are *relationships* and *service*. Our gifts emerge as we live in loving relationship with other believers and with our neighbors. And as we seek to serve others, our gifts will emerge.

A Way of Relating

If we examine all four of the primary passages dealing with the gifts, we find they all speak of the role of the gifts in encouraging and ministering to one another within the context of fellowship. In other words, *our gifts begin to emerge and develop within a relational context.*

In the Romans passage, Paul observed, "Just as each of us has one body with many members, and these members do not all have the same function, so in Christ we who are many form one body, and individually we are members of one another" (Romans 12:4-5). In the Corinthians text: "Now to each one the manifestation of the Spirit is given for the common good" (1 Corinthians 12:7). And Peter teaches, "As each one has received a gift, use the gift to minister to one another, as good stewards of the manifold grace of God" (1 Peter 4:10).

All these passages share one theme: We need each other. You have a gift I need to become complete in Christ.

I have a gift you need. The plans of God are designed to include us both. In relationship we will discover our gifts.

One of the fallacies of some contemporary approaches to gift identification is the implicit assumption that we can discover our gifts outside the context of relationship. I have seen numerous occasions when a church institutes a major program to help people discover and use their gifts only to create a group of people who think they know what their gifts are but are still uninvolved in ministry.

Yet the body of Christ is, indeed, a body. It has members. It is very difficult for an eye to know what it is designed to do without "seeing" itself within the context of an entire body. You could almost imagine a cartoon made up of personalized noses, ears, feet, and legs, looking at each other with total bewilderment when not attached in their proper places to a body.

To discover your gift, enter into significant fellowship with a group of other believers. As you begin to experience life together, situations will arise that will provide opportunities for you to serve the others in your group. For instance, Dan might have administrative gifts that aren't being used in ministry. Another man, Phil, might be having a difficult time trying to help a local youth ministry become more efficient. He might have a tremendous desire to encourage the ministry, and perhaps he even sits on the ministry's board. The problem is, he doesn't have administrative gifting to untangle the mess into which the organization has worked itself.

As Phil and Dan are meeting together, perhaps in a weekly men's group at church, Phil shares his struggle. Immediately, Dan begins to ask questions that Phil has no idea how to answer. Dan begins to see a faulty approach to organization and he considers how it could be remedied. Dan then shares with Phil what he's thinking. Phil might be amazed because Dan's insights haven't even occurred to him. The two men decide to visit the head of the youth ministry, with Dan presenting a few practical suggestions.

The next week in the fellowship group, Dan shares with the other men what happened. One of the other men affirms that he's observed administrative gifts in Dan. The group encourages Dan to continue to explore ways to develop and use his gift. In relationship, one of his gifts has emerged and been identified.

The same principle can help us determine which gifts we *don't* have. Let's say another member of your group, we'll call him Ted, teaches a Sunday school class and is going on vacation for three weeks. He asks if anyone in the group could fill in for him while he is gone. You volunteer. (In a moment I'll show you why this was a very good decision.) For the next three weeks, you teach the young married couples' group at your church. It is unbelievably difficult for you, although you do receive some enjoyment from taking on the task.

During those three weeks, you notice that several couples stop attending, and others have a quizzical look on their faces while you attempt to share certain spiritual gems from the Bible. When Ted returns from vacation, you turn the class over to him. The next week, several of the couples who had left during Ted's absence now return to class.

When your group meets the following week, you talk about your experience. Ted and several of the other men suggest that maybe you don't have the gift of teaching. This is not a judgment on your worth as a human being. It is loving honesty that should free you to pursue your true area of giftedness.

One problem I often see in the church is the lack of a level of relationship in which this kind of honesty can take place. Too often, not wanting to hurt a brother or sister in Christ, we say, "Great job!" when we should say, "I don't think so." A lack of relationship gives faulty reinforcement to a lack of gifting.

You may have heard of the farmer who was working in his field one day when he looked into the sky and saw the letters "PC" formed by the clouds. He immediately assumed that the Lord was calling him to "Preach Christ." He left the farm and began traveling from church to church, attempting to preach the gospel. He was horrible. No one came to know Christ. It was painful to listen to him.

Finally one day, a wise, older Christian took him aside and, in love, told him he needed to go back to the farm. The young man objected and told him how he had seen the letters "PC" in the clouds and believed God was calling him to preach. The loving brother simply smiled, put his arm around the young man's shoulder, and said, "I think He was telling you to 'Plant Corn.'"

Gifts emerge, and are affirmed, in relationship. If you want to discover your gifts, get plugged into a small group and seek to love and minister to the people in the group. They will help you find your place in the body.

A Way of Serving One Another

These stories point to the second key to discovering spiritual gifts—recognizing that *our gifts emerge in the process of exercising them.* This is where we sometimes put the cart before the horse. We often assume we need to know what our gift is in order to figure out where to serve. Eventually, this will be the case, but in the early phases of discovery, there is no substitute for trial and error. All Christians are called to serve, regardless of their gifting. We also tend to be exposed to a wide variety of service opportunities that require a diverse number of gifts. We can take advantage of opportunities at hand to see if they might reveal an area of giftedness.

Dan and Ted discovered administrative potential— and teaching deficiency—through experimentation. How can we come to understand our gifting in any other way? Even most of the tests that attempt to uncover gifts are based on experience and desire. The more exposure and experience we acquire, the more likely we are to nail down our unique set of spiritual gifts. So the old Nike ad, "Just do it!" would be my counsel.

Here is one possible scenario that could develop if we eagerly desire spiritual gifts (see 1 Corinthians 14:1). God will lead us into relationships. We respond by getting involved in fellowship at a more significant level than mere casual acquaintance. In relationship, opportunity and need will come our way. (In all probability, more opportunity and need than we could ever respond to in a lifetime will come our way.) Therefore, as we are walking in the Spirit, we become more sensitive to God tapping us on the shoulder and saying, "Pay attention to this one."

Then some specific need grabs our attention. It pushes a button that connects our deepest motivations and abilities to that situation in a dynamic way. In faith and obedience we choose to step out and see how we might get involved in meeting the need or filling the opportunity. In the midst of serving, we either become energized and receive joy, or the experience drains us and we want out.

Fellow believers observe us serving and either affirm our giftedness to serve in an area or discourage us in this particular area and encourage us to seek other areas of service and need. In the end, we either see that God has used us or we see that our effort has been less than fruitful. We keep at it until we fine tune our understanding of who God created us to be, what our unique gifts and calling are, and the specific areas of service God has designed for us to serve and minister within.

ASSIGNMENT: CHAPTER SIX

Personal Application

1. Read one of the four gifts passages daily (Romans 12:3-8; 1 Corinthians 12:1-11; Ephesians 4:7-13; 1 Peter 4:10-11).
2. Make a list of the gifts you think you might have.
3. Find a ministry need you could become involved in and test your hunch.

Group Discussion

1. Do you agree that God uses "trial and error" to guide us into fruitful service? What is your experience with this? Can you suggest any biblical support for your view?
2. When have you experienced the most excitement or joy in serving? What does this tell you about your gifts?
3. When have you had a real "downer" experience of trying to serve or of being responsible for a particular role in the church? Are you now in a situation of serving that doesn't seem to fit your desires or abilities? What can you do about that? (You might ask for suggestions and advice from the others in your group.)
4. How would you describe the main purpose of spiritual gifts? How well is this purpose being accomplished in your own group or church congregation?
5. If you believe that the spiritual gifts lists are not

exhaustive, what other kinds of gifts might you point to? How have you seen them in action?

6. Spend some time sharing with each other what gifts you have seen at work in one another. Offer suggestions about potential areas of service in the future. Pray for each other that God would open doors to use your gifts.

CHAPTER SEVEN

War in the Spirit

*"For our struggle
is not against flesh and blood."*
—Ephesians 6:12

MY FATHER WAS A VETERAN of World War II,
having served in the 15th Air Force as part of a
B-24 bomber crew. This highly decorated group made
daring forays into enemy held territory and bombed vital
Nazi factories and oil fields. There was no doubt about
their mission, no question that a great evil threatened
the world and must be stopped. Everyone knew who the
enemy was and what was at stake in that war. The soldiers
were heroes; support at home was universal.

How different from the 1960s and 1970s, when U.S.
forces struggled in Vietnam! I was a college student at the

time and didn't know whether the heroic choice was to go to Vietnam or to Canada. Many Americans were so opposed to the war that they burned their draft cards and carried banners declaring, "Hell no, we won't go!" Others proudly displayed bumper stickers advising, "America: Love It or Leave It."

Not only was public opinion sharply divided, but the war itself was very confusing to the soldiers. Many of my friends who fought in Vietnam report how difficult it was to tell friend from foe. The people of Vietnam were engaged in a horrible civil war, not unlike our own, in the sense that both sides looked identical except for their uniforms. Soldiers in the field would enter villages and never know when an apparently friendly villager might turn out to be a North Vietnamese sympathizer— someone who would, at any moment, attempt to put a bullet in them.

WELCOME TO THE REAL WORLD

As confusing as the war in Vietnam was, it cannot compare with the epic spiritual battle in which people of faith must engage on a daily basis. Yes, we are at war! Here the enemy doesn't simply look like the ally. In this conflict, the enemy is invisible and often disguises his attacks in the most subtle types of spiritual camouflage.

To truly understand this war and to fight the fight successfully, we must understand something of the terrain upon which the battle flourishes. We do live in a supernatural universe. reality is more than what we can see or touch. The drama of the visible world is only half of the story.

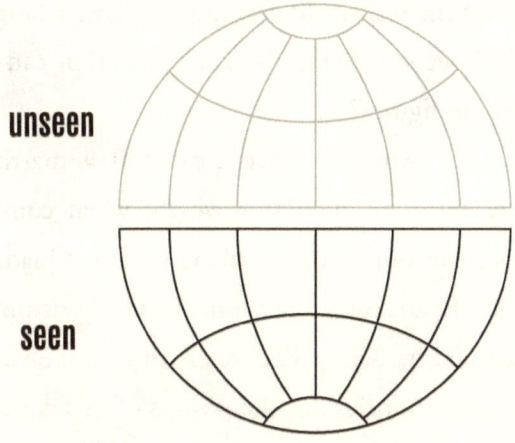

Figure 7.1: The Real World

If the illustration in figure 7.1 contained the totality of the real world, we could divide it in half and label part of the illustration the seen and the other part the unseen.

But along with this division of the *seen* and the *unseen*, the real world is made up of two radically different spiritual realities. Part of the real world, both seen and unseen, is fallen. By this I mean it is disconnected from a vital relationship with God, resulting in massive distortion in the cosmos. On the other hand, part of the real world, both seen and unseen, exists in proper relationship with God. If we use the theological concept of *fallen* to speak of the disconnected sector of reality, we might use the words *redeemed* and *redeeming* to refer to that part of the real world existing in proper relationship to God. A second divider in our illustration can create the reality in figure 7.2.

Suddenly, what we have created is a matrix that illustrates the four quadrants which, when combined, constitute the universe in which we live. Quadrant 1 represents the unseen, fallen dimension of our universe. It is occupied by beings Paul refers to in Ephesians 6 as "rulers . . . authorities . . . the powers of this dark world . . . the spiritual forces of evil in the heavenly realms" (verse 12). This quadrant represents the reality of evil personified. This is the abode of the prince of darkness, the one the Bible calls Satan, or the Devil. He is the enemy in all our spiritual battles.

Quadrant 2 is the part of the matrix representing God and the unseen dimension of His kingdom. From here the Spirit comes to indwell our lives and give us spiritual birth.

Quadrant 3 is that part of reality the Bible calls "the world." It does not represent the physical world, but the operation of the visible universe that is disconnected from a relationship with God. It is seen, but it is fallen.

Quadrant 4 is the part of the matrix representing those who have had a spiritual birth experience. This is the redeemed sector of the universe, called the body of Christ. This is where we "dwell" when we are spiritual men and women.

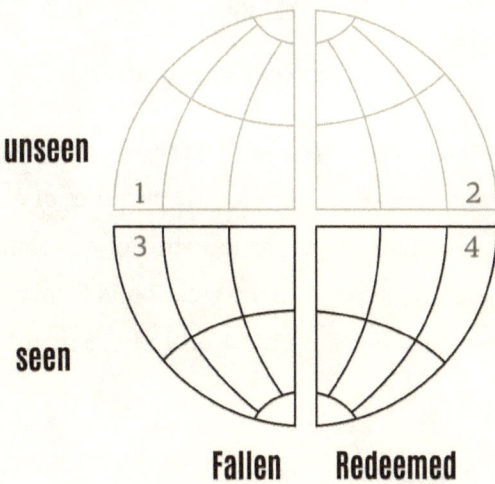

Figure 7.2: The Real World Spiritually

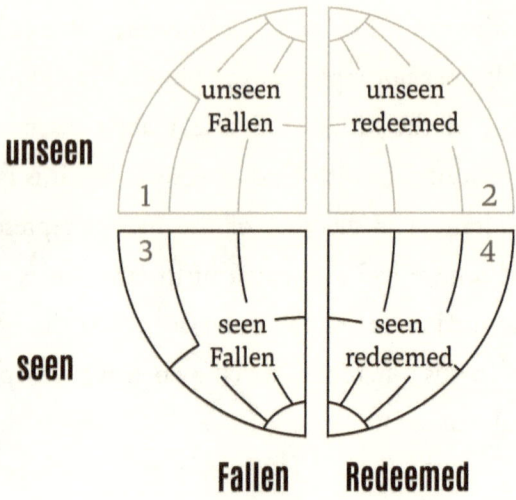

Figure 7.3: Real World Matrix

Spiritual warfare is primarily a result of the inhabitants of quadrant 1 seeking to hinder the purposes of quadrant 2 by launching attack on the residents of quadrant 4 (on you and me). Sometimes that attack comes from quadrant 3, but its origin is always the world of the demonic (see Figure 7.4).

KNOW YOUR ENEMY

As spiritual men and women, we have an enemy. His name is Satan. He is also known as the Devil. Seeking to thwart the plans and purposes of God, he hates us and wants to destroy our lives. If we are going to be effective in the battle, we need to know this enemy and how he operates.

The Bible alludes to the origins of this being in the prophetic books of Isaiah and Ezekiel. Isaiah 14 and Ezekiel 28 paint a portrait of a highly intelligent and marvelously beautiful angel named Lucifer.

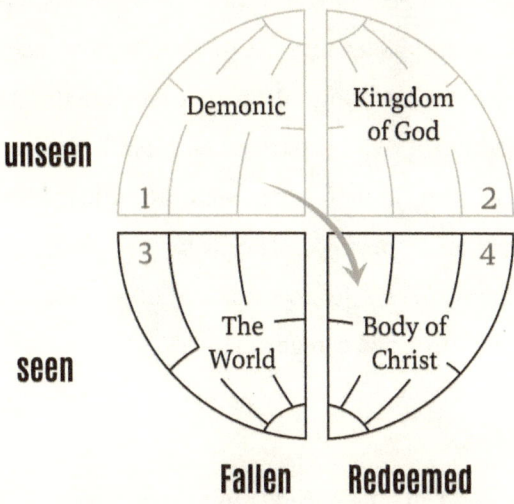

Figure 7.4: Spiritual Warfare

The implication is that his beauty and wisdom corrupted him and he grew "discontent" with living as a servant of God. He wanted to assume the place of God, and rule. His fall shook the Cosmos.

Although not all scholars agree on the meaning of these texts, they seem to give insight into the origin of evil in the universe. These events would precede the fall of humanity recorded in Genesis 3, and they help us understand where the serpent came from. Rulers and authorities, or principalities and powers, refer to a hierarchy of fallen angelic beings we call demons. The book of Revelation hints that perhaps as many as one-third of the entire angelic host followed Satan in his rebellion. This legion and its leader have one primary objective—to thwart the plans of God. On planet Earth, Satan initiates this objective in two primary ways. First, he keeps people from accepting Jesus Christ. Second, he keeps believers as ineffective as possible. The "schemes" Paul speaks of in Ephesians 6:11 refer to these evil objectives, and they tend to fall into two categories.

Deception

The Evil One is a deceiver in so many ways. Consider temptation, for example. It's a form of deception in which we become convinced that we cannot live without that which will ultimately destroy us. Lust and adultery have destroyed many a good man and woman. They have destroyed many a good minister. In retrospect, most of these men and women would agree. But in that moment of passion and temptation, illicit sexual relations became something they couldn't imagine living without.

Seduction is another form of deception and another variation on the theme of temptation. Here the trinkets of this world are made to look more appealing than the rewards of the kingdom of God. Like Esau, we become willing to sell our spiritual birthright for a bowl of lentil soup.

Error is yet another form of deception. Jesus called Satan the "father of lies." From the beginning, Satan has used error as a scheme to accomplish his objectives. Error makes a lie look like true. The great illustration of error is found in the account of the temptation in the garden. God said, "You are free to eat from any tree in the garden; but you must not eat from the tree of the knowledge of good and evil, for when you eat of it you will surely die" (Genesis 2:16-17). That was the truth. Satan came along and said in essence, "You won't die. As a matter of fact, you will be like God." Eve and Adam believed the lie, and the result was disastrous!

One final form of deception Satan uses is accusation. He is called "the accuser of our brethren" in Revelation 12:10. In this case, we come to believe that something we have done cannot be forgiven by the finished work of Christ on the cross.

When accusation is effective, it keeps the believer bound in guilt and discouragement, making him ineffective.

Destruction

The second way the Enemy accomplishes his schemes is by destruction. Jesus painted a vivid contrast between what He came to do and what the Enemy seeks to do in our lives. He said, "The thief [Satan] only comes in order that he might steal and kill and destroy; I have come that they may have life, and have it more abundantly" (John 10:10). What a contrast!

In the book of Revelation, we are told of the day when a horde of demonic beings will be released from an abyss to wreak havoc on the earth. In the ninth chapter, we read that these demonic beings have a king over them whose name in Hebrew is *Abaddon*, and in Greek, *Apollyon*. These words mean "destroyer" and "destruction."

What is Satan out to destroy? Primarily what I call the "foundations." He seeks to destroy those foundational institutions that God has established to accomplish His plans and purposes. Pre-eminent are marriage, the family, and the church. Destructive schemes are at work in the universe to destroy these foundations. The point of these observations is simple. We are at war. It is a spiritual war waged in the heavenlies but played out on earth. The stakes are high—the lives of men, women, boys, and girls. The spiritual man or woman is called to be active and effective in this cosmic conflict. In order for us to be ready, what do we need?

PUT ON THE EQUIPMENT

The primary resource for the spiritual warrior is the Holy Spirit Himself. The indwelling presence of Christ enables us to win this war. Actually, the war was won when Jesus triumphed over these principalities and powers at the cross (Colossians 2:15). For reasons that are not yet apparent, the ultimate victory of Christ has not been realized in the world. God is allowing evil to play out its hand. My conviction is that this decision will be fully vindicated when the final curtain falls on this age. Even the struggle of spiritual warfare will play a role in God's ultimate triumph.

In the meantime, we are being taught an important lesson through the conflict: "Greater is the one who is in you than the one who is in the world" (1 John 4:4). The inner presence of Christ is our greatest asset in the battle. This is why Paul tells us to "be strong in the Lord" (Ephesians 6:10). Every resource we need to fight the good fight is found in Christ.

If you are ever in London, take time to visit the British Museum, where along with some of the oldest fragments of biblical manuscripts in existence, you can actually see every piece of first-century Roman armor displayed. Paul took this common image and attached to each piece a spiritual quality that needs to be present and active in our lives if we are to be effective in spiritual warfare. Just as a Roman soldier would not have thought of going to battle without every piece of his armor in place, we are instructed never to enter the spiritual battlefield without our suit of armor in place. Let's look at the three categories of spiritual armor.

Category #1: God's Word.

Paul calls the Word of God the sword of the Spirit. To fight the battle effectively, we need to be men and women of the Word. God has given His revealed truth to enable us to combat deception. Because deception is one of the two primary categories of Satan's schemes, truth becomes a critical weapon in our arsenal.

The great illustration of this truth comes to us from early in Jesus' ministry. The Gospels tell us that the Spirit led Jesus into the wilderness for forty days, where He was tempted by Satan. At the end of forty days, we see what happened in the final three temptations Jesus faced. Unlike Adam and Eve, Jesus was not deceived. When Satan tempted him, Jesus always replied with the same formula, "It is written" (Luke 4:4,8,12). Three times, the sword of the Spirit shredded the dagger of deception.

If we come to terms with the reality of spiritual warfare and all that is at risk, we would be foolish not to become serious students of God's Word. It is our sword. It is the only weapon we carry. I have been told that the average person in the American church today has less than a sixth-grade level of biblical knowledge. More time is devoted to reading the sports and entertainment sections of the daily paper than to studying and mastering the Scriptures. Yet it's tough to stand against an enemy like the Devil when we're armed with a spiritual peashooter!

Category #2: Christian character.

The second category of armor has to do with our personal character and integrity. Paul identifies the following qualities as pieces of the armor:

1. Truthfulness (our "belt")
2. Righteousness (our "breastplate")
3. Readiness (our "sandals")
4. Faith (our "shield")
5. Salvation (our "helmet")

In the Roman soldier's arsenal, these were the defensive pieces designed to protect him from the enemy's direct attack. If you look closely, you will see that Paul's corollaries are all spiritual character qualities.

The armor is personal holiness. We are most protected from attack when we are "dressed for success." Our wardrobe is simple; we are to be clothed "with the Lord Jesus Christ" (Romans 13:14).

Category #3: Prayer.

Our final resource in spiritual warfare is prayer. In the final three verses of these instructions in Ephesians 6, the word pray occurs six times in one form or another. Paul instructs the Ephesians to "pray in the Spirit at all times" (verse 18). Prayer is a powerful weapon in the battle.

When the disciples asked Jesus to teach them to pray (see Luke 11:1), He responded by giving them a pattern we call the Lord's Prayer. It contains seven phrases of instruction, each of which can help us in developing an effective prayer life. I explore this strategy in detail in my companion book, *Prayer*. It is available on Amazon.

One of the seven components is praying for protection from spiritual attack. Jesus taught the disciples to pray, "deliver us from the evil one" (Matthew 6:13). Some versions translate the instruction as "deliver us from evil." Most of us need little convincing to affirm the reality of evil in the world. The atrocities committed during World War II, not only to the Jewish people of Europe but to millions of other men and women, Christians included, remind us of the depth of malevolent wickedness to which human beings can descend.

And from the Holocaust of Jews in WWII, to the persecution of Christians around the world today, and the demonic massacre of Jews by Hamas on October 7, 2023, we live in a world permeated with evil. But evil is more than an impersonal force. The instructions of Paul in Ephesians 6 and the teaching of Jesus in the Gospels alert us to the fact of personalized evil in the universe. The Greek text of the Lord's Prayer contains the definite article "the" before the word *poneros*, translated "evil." The use of the article points to personification. Jesus is teaching us to pray for deliverance from the Devil.

In prayer, we not only put on armor, we actually erect a spiritual fortress around our lives. The word *deliver* can mean "protect" or "defend." Throughout the history of Israel, God was pictured as a fortress against the enemy. One of the more vivid images of this kind of protection is the agricultural concept of a hedge.

During biblical times, the resources for fence-building were often unavailable, so farmers would plant a dense hedge around their crops as protection against predators. God used this agricultural picture to teach Israel about His protection. In the fifth chapter of Isaiah, we have a passage called "The Song of the Vineyard." Here God tells of planting a metaphorical vineyard, representing the nation of Israel. Then He speaks of placing a hedge around it to protect it. The passage is a warning of the coming Babylonian invasion that will destroy rebellious Israel. God said, "I will remove its hedge, and it will be destroyed" (Isaiah 5:5). This image also occurs in the book of Job. In poetic fashion Job presents an encounter in the heavenly arena where the true war is being waged. Satan appears in the presence of God, and God draws his attention to Job, who is "blameless and upright" (Job 1:8). The accuser of the brethren responds by observing that God has placed a "hedge" around Job. It is the removal of this protection that gives Satan the opportunity, for God's hidden purposes, to afflict Job.

We can put up a "hedge" around our lives and families. In modern technological terms we might speak of a spiritual force field or grid. The protective power is the very presence of God Himself. He is the refuge. His presence and power make up the hedge. When we pray for deliverance from the Evil One, God activates the force field.

I find it helpful to use this imagery when I pray. I ask God to activate the hedge of His power and presence around my life and my family. I pray that if, by any of my actions or neglect, I have created a "breach" in the protection, God would shore up that breach. I also pray that He would drive out whatever predators have invaded my "vineyard."

One final aspect of prayer lends itself to our protection in spiritual battle. Because Satan is a finite being, he is only able to be in one place at one time. He can only personally attack a limited number of men and women, and I'm quite sure that I'm not significant enough to merit his personal attention. That means that my struggle is probably against lesser "principalities and powers." I am the object of demonic attack in the war.

Demons are fallen angels. If a fallen angel is going to attack me, I would like to have one of the Lord's host around to stand in the gap. I believe in the ministry of angels. I believe it because the Bible teaches it. The psalmist declared that God will give His angels charge over us (Psalm 91:11). This promise comes within the context of God being our refuge (verse 9). The book of Hebrews teaches that angels are ministering spirits sent to serve those who have come to know Christ (Hebrews 1:14).

We live in an era of renewed interest in angels. Much of that interest is coming from traditions outside the mainstream of orthodox faith and, to be honest, that makes me nervous. Satan has the ability to disguise himself as an "angel of light" (2 Corinthians 11:14). Therefore, I fear that much of the so-called "angelic" activity heralded these days could actually be demonic deception.

A careful reading of the Gospels and the book of Acts should alert us to the fact that authentic angelic activity is probably taking place all around us, all of the time. In prayer, I ask God to send for the members of the host assigned to me and my family. I have to admit, I don't fully understand this subject, but I believe that God answers prayer for angelic help. With the Spirit at work within me, and the armor of God in place, with the sword of the Spirit in hand, and a life invested in prayer, we can be men and women who experience the victory of Christ in our lives. In other words, we can be effective members of God's kingdom.

In this and the previous chapters we have explored the seven primary areas of the person and work of the Holy Spirit. Understanding and applying these truths will help you become a spiritual man or woman. In the next chapter, we'll consider what it might look like in real life if we put these principles into practice. I've included several "snapshots" of people's daily lives; people like you and me, who are trying to put it all together.

ASSIGNMENT: CHAPTER 7

Personal Application

1. Read Ephesians 6 every day this week.
2. Memorize Ephesians 6:12.
3. Evaluate your armor. Where are you strong? Where do you need work?

Group Discussion

1. Talk about the strengths and weaknesses in your armor.
2. What is your conception of who Satan is? What is the danger of underemphasizing the biblical truths about him?
3. Is it possible to become too preoccupied with the Devil? Explain.
4. Do you normally think of your life as being lived out on a battlefield? Explain.
5. What, for you, is the best thing about prayer? What is the most confusing or frustrating thing?
6. What part of the Christian armor is the most difficult for you to put on—and keep on? Why?
7. Do you agree that most believers spend more time with the daily paper than with the Word? Where are you in this regard? Is reading and studying the Bible something that comes easily for you? What helps motivate you to spend time in the Word?

8. What has been your experience in the past with "spiritual warfare"? Share an incident in your life that you believe was spiritual warfare.

9. How, specifically, could you become more effective in fighting your daily battles? What first steps could you take this week to become more effective?

10. Pray for group members' areas of susceptibility to attack.

CHAPTER 8

A DAY IN THE SPIRIT

"This is the day the Lord has made."
—Psalm 118:24

WHAT ARE THE PEOPLE IN YOUR fellowship group like during the week? Have you ever wanted to look into their daily lives to see how they compare with your attempts to let the Spirit reign? Perhaps you'd see something like this:

6:30 a.m.—At the home of Jim Gonzales, history teacher . . . "And Lord, again I ask you to fill me with your Spirit . . . amen," Jim concludes, after spending fifteen minutes reading the Bible and praying. Getting up from his knees, Jim looks at the clock and realizes he'd better hop in the shower and get dressed for work. Walking from the living room to the bathroom, he thinks about what he'd just read in his Bible.

In the previous weeks he'd been reading a book, *The Spirit*, given to him by a friend. Jim had studied the book, chapter by chapter, and had completed the weekly assignments. The result was a deeper understanding of who the Holy Spirit is and of all the Spirit was doing in his life. The study had also created within Jim a deep desire to be a man of the Spirit.

Today Jim had decided he would attempt to be conscious throughout the day of putting into practice the newly learned principles. The first step in that process had been to end his time alone with God by asking the Holy Spirit to fill and control him. As he walked down the hall toward the shower, Jim sensed that God was going to honor that prayer and teach him valuable lessons about the practical realities of being a spiritual man.

8:30 a.m.—*At the office of Jill McCann, accountant . . .*

As she arrived at her office, Jill McCann was struck by how many of the principles she had been studying in the last few weeks came into play during an average day's work. As an employee of a small accounting firm, Jill had people surrounding her in the customer end of the operations, as well as at the office. Over the preceding weeks, she'd been thinking about how her life affected a multitude of relationships on a daily basis. It was Monday morning, and that meant staff meeting.

These meetings involved all the senior-level personnel, including Rod, owner and CEO of the company. The meetings weren't Jill's favorite part of the week. Business was good, but the meetings were still stressful. Not all of the relationships around the table were in good shape. There tended to be a bit of competition between the various accountants, and that spirit was fostered by Rod, who saw it as a way of keeping production at the highest levels.

A few minutes into the meeting, Jill sensed that things were deteriorating. Lou and Jill held similar positions, but Lou had a way of pushing her buttons at times—and Jill's buttons were taking a brutal hit at the moment. The group had to make a decision about who would handle a new client and who would have to travel to the nearby town of Castle Rock to work with an established client. As the discussion developed, it became obvious that everyone wanted to stay in town, and Lou was listing all the reasons why he should work on the local hospital account. Jill's stomach started knotting up. *What's the problem here?* As Lou talked, Jill reflected on what she had learned about that part of her inner life the Bible called the flesh. Irritability seemed to be one of the main products flowing from this part of her internal landscape. Nowhere was this more the case than in her relationship with Lou.

Patience. The word came into Jill's mind as she considered what resource she needed to combat the negative emotions rising within her. She silently prayed, *Lord, I need the fruit of the Spirit. I'm not patient by nature, but I know You can help.* Jill remembered that she had a part to play in the process of bearing fruit. Be patient, was the command that came to mind. In this case, she decided to keep her mouth shut, instead of responding to Lou's lame arguments.

10:30 a.m.—At the office of Rich Stevenson, lawyer . . .

Ann Wendall knocked at precisely 10:30. Rich looked up and smiled as she walked into the office. Ann's job at the company was to handle complaints coming in from clients. She was a very nice lady; however, for Rich, and his attempt to be a man of the Spirit, she was also an extremely attractive temptation. Rich had been through some tough stretches in his marriage, but he and his wife were enjoying the benefits of sticking it out and working through the hard times. Yet it always amazed him that no matter how good things were going on the home front, an attractive woman still stirred his blood and presented a challenge to his thought life.

Ann sat in the chair across from him and placed a file on the edge of the desk. As she reported a complaint that would probably require hours of review, Rich worked at processing his internal struggle with the provocative clothing and natural beauty before him. He had been reading the book *The Spirit*, and the thought that kept running through his mind was, *the lust of the flesh.*

Rich knew the Spirit had created a new reality in his life and that thought was tremendously encouraging. His life before Christ had been pretty tough. Old habits were dying a slow and painful death. Recognizing the normative nature of this conflict had been a major source of enlightenment for Rich.

At the moment, the battle involved his eyes and the shape under Ann's sweater. "The good news is that conflict is normative." He recalled those words from the chapter in the book on the struggle with the flesh. Okay, he thought. *It's normal, but what comes next?*

As he zeroed in on the complaint at hand and the details required to address the problem, Rich hardly noticed the time flying by. When Ann left the office, a full thirty minutes had elapsed. As he thought about that, another observation came into his consciousness. During the entire period he had focused on the task at hand, not on Ann. The conscious act of identifying the action of the flesh and diverting his attention away from Ann's figure had lifted him over the hurdle of unwholesome thinking. *Could it be this easy?* He remembered the verse he and his buddies were memorizing in their small group: "I made a covenant with my eyes not to look lustfully at a woman" (Job 31:1). It might seem like a small victory for some men, but for Rich it was a huge triumph of God's grace.

11:30 a.m.—*Brad Dorn, at ProGuard Roofing Company*
. . .

His crew needed to be on the road by noon. The job of repairing the roof of a small laundry downtown wasn't exceptionally challenging. The real challenge for Brad Dorn was providing his diverse crew of workers with the kind of leadership and management that best facilitated the job. A new dynamic had been added in recent weeks. Now this leadership task was to be done in the Spirit. Brad wasn't sure how that would look.

The trucks were kept in the storage yard, and Brad had arranged to meet his men there. As he approached, he saw Luis and Arturo—second-generation legal immigrants who had been with the company for five years. They worked hard, and Brad got along with both of them. They were sitting on some concrete blocks, eating homemade food out of classic lunch pails.

Brad could see Randy inside one of the trucks. He was the white supremacist on the crew and Brad had a tough time handling him. Randy was constantly giving the rest of the crew "an attitude," and Brad had to call him on it regularly.

The final member of the crew was also the newest. His name was Martin, and he was African-American. Brad had grown to enjoy the young man's company because Martin was a believer, too. He usually rode with Brad to the job site, and the two frequently talked about their faith.

What a crew! Brad thought, as he walked up to the trucks. It was a microcosm of America, with all the challenges a racially mixed group presents.

"Hi, guys," he said.

A mumbled "Hi, Boss" greeted him from all but Randy, who simply gave a little salute as he stuffed a few more Burger King fries into his mouth.

On the way to the job, Brad and Martin talked about trying to live in the Spirit throughout this one day.

"When you think of it," Martin observed, "that's what every day is supposed to be."

"Yeah, but I think I need to take it a day at a time," Brad said.

"How's it going so far?" Martin asked.

"Great. But I really haven't had too much of a challenge. It's been a pretty smooth day, so far."

They had been working on the roof of the laundry for about two hours when the trouble started. Although it should have been an easy job, it turned out to be tricky. They were tackling a timeworn roof that had multiple layers of vintage asphalt. All that old built-up material had to be torn off before the actual repairs could begin.

Frustration levels were rising, and Randy had persisted in giving Luis and Arturo a hard time. Brad didn't see it begin, but he heard Luis yell something in Spanish. He turned just in time to see Randy land a sneaky left hook to Arturo's chin. The dazed man went down, and Brad—before he was even aware of what he was doing—flew across the roof, slamming Randy with an NFL-worthy hit.

Raw rage seethed and boiled over. Months of anger had been brewing against Randy, and Brad felt himself getting ready to smash him in the face.

Then he stopped. He became conscious of what he was about to do.

No. This isn't right.

The look in Randy's eyes reminded Brad of a deer paralyzed in somebody's headlight beams. Like most bullies, Randy didn't know what to do when a guy stood up to him. Under the shaved head and the Nazi tattoos was a confused and scared kid. All these thoughts flooded Brad's mind as he held Randy down on the roof.

Help, Lord. It was all he could think to pray. A calm washed over him. He became aware of the rate of his heartbeat, and the tension wracking his body. Pulling Randy to his feet, Brad considered what he should do next. *Give me wisdom, Lord.*

"Go home, Randy," Brad heard himself say.

"That little wet—", Rand started.

"Don't say a thing," Brad intervened.

"Yeah, but . . . "

"No 'buts' about it. You're through for the day, and if you can't come back tomorrow with a better attitude, then don't come back."

Randy grabbed his gear and headed for the ladder. The rest of the crew stood watching, stunned. Brad sat down on the roof as soon as Randy was far enough down the ladder that he couldn't see him.

"You all right, Boss?" Luis asked.

Brad nodded. "Yeah . . . I just need to pull it back together."

You guys get back to work and try to finish this puppy up."

"You bet, amigo," Luis responded.

"Are you okay?" This time it was Martin.

"Yeah. I'm just a little shook. I almost smashed his face in."

"You would have been justified," Martin said.

"Maybe, but that wouldn't make it right."

Martin thought about that for a moment, then picked up a lump of old tar and threw it to the ground. "Go take a break, and I'll make sure we get this thing put to bed."

Brad climbed down the ladder and headed for the truck. He was glad he'd asked Martin to park where the shade would cover the truck in the afternoon. He opened the door and sat down in the front seat to think about all that had just happened. Two facts struck him. First, Randy had a real problem. All this white supremacist idiocy had the smell of evil. Second, what about his response to Randy? How much of what had just happened was a "spiritual event"?

On the one hand, Brad realized that his anger had flared. Rage was a problem he had dealt with periodically. It was one of the deeds of the flesh he had learned about in a book he was reading. It was also sin, however justifiably provoked. That meant that in a split second his ego had taken over and responded to the old nature and its vicious bent. Brad confessed that he had usurped the throne; then he invited Jesus to take control again.

For a few minutes he thought through all the dynamics at work in the incident. Was Randy influenced by Satan to harass and finally attack Arturo? How about his own response? What triggered the rage? In real life, all this was so complex. He spent a few minutes praying. He thanked Jesus for His forgiveness and asked the Holy Spirit to fill him. He also thanked the Lord that He had stopped him before punching Randy. While he was at it, Brad prayed for spiritual protection again and also prayed that God would work in Randy's life. *"And give me an opportunity to talk to him about You, Lord. . . ."*

4:00 p.m.—*Starbuck's*

Sharon Yamamoto met with her small group on Wednesday afternoons. She was glad she would have some fellow believers to help her "debrief" the events of her day. The whole group had been studying the book *The Spirit* and had agreed to hold each other accountable as they tried to apply what they were learning. This would be an interesting meeting.

The group met at the Starbuck's. Along with Sharon, there was Joyce, a local graphic designer; Linda, an attorney; and Meg, a stay at home mom. The four had met at a women's retreat two years previously, and had gotten together weekly ever since. The coffee shop was quiet and relatively private at this time of day.

"I've had a wild one," Sharon said, after the small talk died down. "I think Mark almost called it quits today."

Sharon went on to tell the group it was one of those marital discussions in which a small conflict suddenly turns into a major brawl. Mark and Sharon had been helping their daughter, Stephanie, get ready for her senior trip. Stephanie needed her class sweatshirt for several events on the trip but had loaned it to one of her friends. The sweatshirt in question had still not been returned, and Mark was getting impatient with their daughter.

That's when Sharon made the mistake of intervening. She told the group about her suggestion that maybe enough energy had gone into reminding Stephanie about the sweatshirt . . . and how well it had been received.

Not well.

Then Mark suggested that perhaps Sharon didn't need to be involved in the discussion at all.

That was the point at which Sharon told Mark exactly what he could do with the sweatshirt in question, and she left the house. Mark had called her at work and told her she didn't need to come home until she learned to stop being verbally abusive.

When the group's conversation turned to analysis, the women all agreed that the spiritual principles they'd studied were at work all the time, in all kinds of combinations. The other women felt as though Sharon had experienced both a spiritual warfare episode and a "flesh attack." Other women told of incidents during the week that seemed to involve similar issues. Together, the women committed to pray for each other about how they could be Spirit-filled around their husbands and children. Sharon agreed to confess to her husband that she had been "in the flesh" and to ask for forgiveness.

After sharing war stories for a while, talk turned to the issue of spiritual gifts. As a group, the women had decided to help each other identify their individual gifts and explore ways to exercise them. Linda was teaching an adult Sunday school class at her church and asked Meg if she would consider filling in for her the next week.

"Do you think I might have a teaching gift?" Meg asked with a joking attitude.

"Actually, I suspect you do," Linda replied. "That's why I'd like you to fill in for me."

"You're kidding." Meg looked surprised.

"I think so, too," Sharon said. "You think like a teacher."

"I'm housewife," Meg responded.

"Hey, quit putting yourself down," Joyce said. "You're smart, and you know it. You study the Bible more than any of us, and you're always coming up with insights that none of the rest of us got out of our study. You've really helped me to understand about the Spirit, a topic that's always been confusing to me."

"You also do a good job of telling us what you're learning," Linda said. "It seems like that's what a good teacher does. They study the Bible, and then share what they have learned in a way that makes sense and helps their students."

"I never thought of it like that," Meg said. "But the book said we ought to be open to trial and error, so why not?"

"I think I'll come and check you out," Sharon said. "I might have a gift of discernment and be able to tell you whether you should 'preach Christ' or 'plant corn.'" Everyone got a kick out of that.

The ladies spent part of their time together talking about what everyone's gifts might be. They used the last fifteen minutes of their time to pray for each other, asking that the Holy Spirit would fill and control their lives and help them to be more conscious of when ego takes over again. Sharon headed home to try to work out her relationship with Mark. *Hopefully, he has the gift of mercy*, Sharon thought to herself

6:00 p.m.—*At the home of Tim Archer, record store manager* . . . There's that blasted bike—again! As Tim pulled into the driveway, he couldn't believe he was going to have to get out and move Robbie's bike before pulling into the garage. Yet this was where the rubber met the road. However else he had learned reading *The Spirit*, if it didn't work at home, it didn't work.

Tim and Barb had been married for thirteen years. Except for a few glitches in the first year, and a tough stretch at the famous seven-year itch point, they had built a good marriage. Robbie was their only child, an eleven-year-old going on twenty-five. Parents were always prejudiced, he guessed, but Tim figured Robbie was a budding genius. He loved computers, music, and surfing. Living near the ocean was a great blessing, and Tim never failed to be grateful.

He walked into the house and took in the blast of guitar riffs coming from down the hall and the smell of garlic bread cooking in the kitchen.

"I'm home from the war," he announced. It was his usual greeting when it had been a hard day.

"Hi, Babe," came a greeting from the kitchen.

Tim entered the kitchen where his wife was fixing spaghetti for dinner. He walked over and gave her a hug, and a kiss on the cheek.

"How are you doing?" he asked, as he always did. "Great!" was Barb's enthusiastic response. She obviously had enjoyed a nice day. It wasn't always like this, but Jim was glad she was in such a good mood.

"How about your day?" she asked.

"Challenging," Tim replied.

"How's that?" Barb asked, as she carried the spaghetti noodles to the kitchen table.

"I think I'm getting burned-out on the music business."

"You're kidding."

"Nope. Today I found myself wondering if God might not want me to do something else with my life. Then I thought about how tight our finances always seem to be and how I probably couldn't get a job any better than the one I have at the store. Anyway, the long and short of it is that I'm feeling a bit trapped and discouraged."

Barb looked at him with an understanding look on her face. "Hi, Dad!" The conversation was interrupted by Robbie's entrance.

Tim reached out and grabbed his son and gave him a hug. "Hi, Son."

"Hey, Dad, you've gotta hear this song I'm writing. I figured out how to play everything on my guitar that I can play on the piano, and then I started writing a song to go with the video game I'm going to create when I finish learning how to do programming."

The words came out so fast, with such bubbly enthusiasm, that Tim had to keep from cracking up and laughing.

"Great! I can't wait to hear it, Robbie."

Over dinner, Tim shared more about how he was feeling. The three of them talked about what the book *The Spirit* had said about the complexity of living a Spirit-filled life. Barb was wondering if Tim's new sensitivity to the Holy Spirit might be playing some part in his struggle at work. Robbie had some questions about spiritual warfare and about what Tim and Barb thought demons might look like. His questions made Tim aware that even at age eleven there is a great deal of interest in the supernatural. Almost every cartoon show on television seemed to have supernatural creatures or aliens. Tim thought he needed to keep closer track of the things Robbie was watching.

When it looked as though dinner was about to end, Tim sensed that the Lord was trying to get his attention. The thought *If it doesn't work at home, it doesn't work* came back into his mind. He looked over at the kitchen and thought about how it would be a nice thing to help Barb clean it up. Then he realized it wouldn't be just a nice thing, it would be a kind thing—maybe even a good thing. What was that word? *Chrestotes?* Something like that. He also became aware of the fact that what he really wanted to do was stretch out on the couch and read the paper.

Love is decision and action. The fruit of the Spirit is love. Be kind. Do good. All these phrases ran through his mind. *Lord, empower me to serve.* No lightning; no thunder. Not even a strong desire to do anything came over him. But he knew he was supposed to help. He rose from his chair and carried their plates to the sink, where he proceeded to rinse them and put them in the dishwasher. He then started cleaning the kitchen.

"You don't have to do that," Barb said from the table. "I'll get it later."

"Let me help you get a jump on it," Tim said.

He worked for about fifteen minutes, cleaning everything he felt competent to clean. When he finished, he felt he'd done what he was supposed to do. Fruit had been produced.

8:33 p.m.—*At the home of Bob Jones, landscaper . . .*

After a lonely dinner, Bob settled into his favorite recliner in front of the television. He opened a beer and turned to the NBA play-off game. Next to the chair sat a copy of a book several of the men from church were reading. His friend Brad had given it to him and suggested Bob might find it helpful. The book had something to do with the Holy Spirit. Bob had read a few pages and decided he didn't need it.

Two hours and four beers later, Bob woke up in the chair, and then headed for the bedroom for the night. It sure seemed quiet around the house since Margaret had moved out.

10:00 p.m.—*At the home of Brad Dorn . . .*

It was around ten o'clock when the phone rang. Linda answered, and from the look on her face, Brad could tell it was something important.

"Randy, for you," Linda said.

Brad walked to the phone and sat down in the chair next to it. "Hi, Randy," he said with as little emotion as possible.

"Boss, I'd like to apologize for today," Randy began. It was strange to hear Randy call him "Boss." Usually only Luis or Arturo addressed him that way.

"I don't know what came over me. I'm really sorry, and I'd like to come back to work tomorrow."

"Randy," Jim began, "you know I'll accept your apology, but would you mind if I made a few ground rules for you?"

There was a moment of silence on the other end of the line, and then Randy said, "Okay."

"Let me begin by apologizing to you for losing my cool," Brad said. "I'd like to ask you to forgive me for knocking you down and almost slugging you."

"Hey, I deserved it. I'm just glad you didn't hit me," Randy said.

"Me, too. I actually was trying to go through the day in the Spirit, and I blew it."

"What do you mean?" Randy asked.

Brad had never talked to any of the other men on the crew about his faith, except for Martin. He knew Randy wasn't exactly the religious type, but he had prayed for Randy just this afternoon. He began to sense the Holy Spirit prompting him to talk about Jesus.

"A couple of years ago I became a Christian," Brad began.

"I know you and Martin both go to church and stuff," Randy said.

"Becoming a Christian is a lot more than going to church," Brad said. "It's a commitment to Jesus Christ as your Boss," he joked spontaneously. "But lately I've been trying to let Him have more control of my life. I was trying to make it through the whole day without fouling it up. When I let loose on you, I was so mad I really wanted to hit you," he said honestly.

"I could tell you were pretty steamed, but I don't blame you," Randy replied.

"I believe the Holy Spirit helped me," Brad said.

"I'm not sure what that means," Randy said.

"The Holy Spirit is like Jesus in you," Brad said. "He helps you live for God from the inside out. He is the one who gives you the ability to do what the Lord wants you to do."

"Sometimes I think I could use something like that," Randy said.

Brad was surprised. He never would have thought Randy might be interested in spiritual things.

"We all do, Randy. You can have it, if you want it. I think Jesus could help you not be so angry with everyone."

"Yeah? Well, I'll think about it."

When it seemed as if Randy had probably had as much as he could handle, Brad backed off. He was glad he'd shared as much as he had. Maybe it would open the door for future discussions. *Wouldn't that be amazing!* Brad thought. *Randy coming to Christ. But I guess nothing is impossible with God.*

10:35 p.m.—Still at Brad's house . . .

It was time to turn off the lights. Linda had already drifted off to sleep, but Brad had spent a few minutes reading from the book he'd been slowly savoring at night. It was Frederick Buechner's latest novel, *On the Road with the Archangel.* Buechner was one of Brad's favorite authors. This book was based on a story from the Catholic version of the Bible, in one of the books of the Apocrypha. Throughout the novel, Buechner referred to God as "the Holy One," and Brad was reflecting on how great the Holy One is.

It had been a good day. Pretty typical, except for the fight with Randy. Had he walked in the Spirit? As far as he could tell, it was something of a mixed bag. He had slipped into the old ways a few times, but whenever he became aware that he needed the Holy Spirit to take control, he had relinquished and invited the Spirit to take over. Had he been filled with the Spirit? By faith, yes. Had he borne fruit? It seemed that in his relationships at home and in the way he'd handled his failure at work, the product had been good. Had he used his gifts? He wasn't so sure. Had he experienced spiritual warfare? Definitely! Had he experienced the conflict between the flesh and the Spirit? All day long.

Brad reached over and set the alarm. Fifteen minutes early—like the last seven weeks. If this day had reinforced anything for him, it was the need for time alone with God and time to study the Bible. *Putting on the armor for the day.* That was Brad's last thought as he drifted off to sleep.

ASSIGNMENT: CHAPTER 8

Group Discussion

1. How realistic, or unrealistic, did you find the vignettes in this chapter? Explain.

2. Which man or woman could you relate to the most? Why? The least? Why?

3. To what extent have you allowed the Spirit to be in control when you are at work? What difference can that make?

4. If you had been Brad on the roof with Randy, how would you have handled the situation?

5. How could the Spirit play a role in your own marital "discussions"—like the one between Frank and Marcie?

6. Choose one of the men's stories and offer an alternative ending. Tell how things might have worked out if that man were you.

7. Now that you are through studying this book, what is the next step for you as a group?

ABOUT THE AUTHOR

Photo by Kenn Bisio

ob Beltz is a minister, teacher, author and film producer. As an ordained minister in the Evangelical Presbyterian Church, Bob was co-founder and Teaching Pastor of Cherry Hills Community Church in Denver, Colorado. He was Senior Pastor of High

Street Community Church in Santa Cruz, California, and Senior Pastor of Highline Community Church in Greenwood Village, Colorado.

Bob went to University of Missouri where he earned his bachelor's degree, then moved to Denver where he earned his Master of Arts and Doctor of Ministry degrees from Denver Seminary.

Bob is the President of the Telos Project, a not-for-profit corporation working to impact contemporary culture with biblical truth. In this capacity, he has helped develop, produce, and market films for the Anschutz Film Group, parent company of Walden Media (*The Lion, the Witch, and the Wardrobe, Prince Caspian, The Voyage of the Dawn Treader, Because of Winn-Dixie*) and Bristol Bay Productions (*Ray, Sahara*). Bob was the Associate Producer of Crusader Entertainment's film *Joshua*, based on Joseph Girzone's best-selling novel, and helped develop and produce *Amazing Grace: the William Wilberforce Story*. Working with Mark Burnett and Roma Downey, Bob was the Associate Producer of the Emmy nominated *The Bible* Series on the History Channel, *AD: the Bible Continues* on NBC, and the movie *Son of God*.

Bob lives in Castle Pines, Colorado with his wife, Joy. He is the father of two children, Stephanie and Baker, and grandfather of two grandchildren, Jaxon and Katt.

Bob is the best-selling author of twenty books:

1. Daily Disciplines for the Christian Man
2. Real Christianity
3. Becoming a Man of Prayer
4. Prayer: A Strategy Based on the Lord's Prayer
5. Becoming a Man of the Spirit
6. Becoming a Man of the Word
7. The Word: Understanding and Enjoying the Bible
8. The Solomon Syndrome
9. The Solomon Syndrome (revised and updated)
10. Transforming Your Prayer Life
11. Somewhere Fast
12. Lilith Redeemed
13. Me and McCartney
14. She Loves You
15. How to Survive the End of the World
16. Revelation Explained
17. World Changers
18. Accountability Among Men
19. The Road to Somewhere
20. The Spirit: Who He is and What He Does

www.bobbeltz.com